CountryLiving

Christmas Joys

HEARST BOOKS
New York

An Imprint of Sterling Publishing
1166 Avenue of the Americas
New York, NY 10036

Design By: Susan Uedelhofen

ISBN 978-1-61837-194-2

Designed by Susan Uedelhofen

Distributed in Canada by Sterling Publishing
c/o Canadian Manda Group, 664 Annette Street
Toronto, Ontario, Canada M6S 2C8
Distributed in Australia by Capricorn Link (Australia) Pty. Ltd.
P.O. Box 704, Windsor, NSW 2756, Australia

For information about custom editions, special sales, and premium and corporate purchases, please contact Sterling Special Sales at 800-805-5489 or specialsales@sterlingpublishing.com.

Manufactured in China

2 4 6 8 10 9 7 5 3 1

www.sterlingpublishing.com

CountryLiving

Christmas Joys

DECORATING, CRAFTS & RECIPES

HEARST BOOKS
New York

PART 3
Recipes for Celebrations

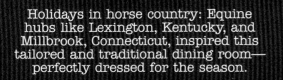

Holidays in horse country: Equine hubs like Lexington, Kentucky, and Millbrook, Connecticut, inspired this tailored and traditional dining room—perfectly dressed for the season.

While there's plenty to love about summer, spring, and fall, no season gets our editors' creative juices flowing like Christmas. The smells, the sounds, the sights—the whole Yuletide is a feast for the senses (as well as a literal feast— hello, holiday buffet table!). So it was our infinite pleasure to put together our very favorite holiday ideas for decorating, handmade gifts, parties, dinners, and desserts (including cookies!) and serve them up to you in the pages that follow. They're the kind of ideas you've come to expect from **Country Living**—humble rather than fancy, simple rather than complicated, drawing on the rich tradition of our nation's agrarian past—yet somehow they bring home the spirit of the season like nothing else. We hope you enjoy them—and the very happiest of holidays.

–Rachel Hardage Barrett,
editor-in-chief, Country Living

Seasonal style: Liberated from their shiny foil-wrapped pots, poinsettias put on a more contemporary show.

PART
ONE

Very Merry Decorating

Sometimes evergreens look best au naturel, especially when stationed outdoors on a porch or patio.

Holiday House Tours

The Christmas spirit can glow in every part of your residence—from the front porch and foyer to the living and dining rooms, right down to bedrooms, baths, and beyond (even the crafts room!). Let the easy, honest, unpretentious, and thoroughly charming ideas on the pages that follow inspire you to bring happy holiday décor to your own home this year.

SEASON'S GREETINGS!

The front porch is the first part of your home people see. Say "come on in" with greenery wreaths, stacks of firewood, and other symbols of good cheer. Choose styles in sync with your abode—rustic for a cabin, more polished for a classic clapboard.

A gift-bedecked weathered blue bench harmonizes perfectly with the unfinished wood exterior of this one-room cabin in Tennessee. Above, an outsized pinecone wreath.

Assorted blankets and birch logs offer visitors a warm welcome.

A red door is cheery all year round but it's perfect at Christmastime. Evergreens in bright-orange planters and a wreath on the pediment make a holiday statement.

READY FOR COMPANY

Anyone who walks through your front door (including you!) will feel merry and bright when the entry to your home is decked out in holiday attire. Evergreens and wreaths are traditional outdoor décor, but winter sports equipment like sleds and snowshoes are more unexpected options.

A pair of cast cement urns from a flea market and a vintage sled flank this traditional front door.

BRIGHT IDEA! Tuck sprigs and berries inside a trapper's basket for a fresh twist on the wreath.

RED, WHITE, AND BRIGHT

If the porch and front door give visitors a first impression of your home, the entryway offers the second. It's where people stop, stamp the snow off their feet, and catch their breath. Amp up the hospitality with greenery, stockings, and other décor, like the wintery secondhand painting opposite.

A simple pine wreath made by a local crafter and a demilune table from Ikea topped with a plain wooden tiered server bring Scandinavian style to this northern Wisconsin foyer.

An entryway bench with beadboard backing is just the right place for a stocking (and jacket and hat) to be hung with care.

A 70-year-old clam-shucking table, once used in an Atlantic City seafood restaurant, now resides in a Connecticut home, holding amaryllises and paperwhites.

WELCOMING TOUCHES

When the holidays roll around, dress your regular foyer décor in festive attire. Go simple, with a single pine sprig in a plain vase, or splash out with an array of potted blooms. (Stick with a single shade for maximum impact.) Homemade ornaments dangling in front of a mirror reflect well on all who enter.

The painted dresser, vintage lamp, poster, and ephemera on the wall work year-round, but a simple pine sprig and pretty gifts mean it's Christmastime.

A console and antiques-store mirror are joined by a wreath on the adjacent door and handmade ornaments.

BRIGHT IDEA! Fashion ornaments like these by stamping kraft-paper rectangles.

{11}

The hearth in this living room lacks a mantel, so stockings are hung from a length of twine. Easy!

HOMESPUN HOLIDAY

A tree decked out in shades of gold, white, and blue, and stockings made of natural fabric fit right in to this home's "high country casual" decorating style, where fine pieces are brought together with more rustic elements. The armchair dates from the 1930s. The child's table and antique ebonized mirror hail from Sweden.

A small tree atop a mahogany-veneer sideboard is decorated in glass ornaments limited to a palette of blue, green, and gold. Beneath, presents are wrapped in matching paper.

{14}

BLUE CHRISTMAS

No one ever said holiday décor has to be nonstop red and green. In this home, blue nudges red aside and greens sometimes tend toward lime. Even the wreaths on the bare windows are made of juniper and blue spruce. On the coffeetable, white amaryllis tinged with grean and bowls of blue and green ornaments and candies repeat the color theme.

Finnish birch and felt ornaments were used to trim the tree in this Scandinavian-inspired home.

OH SO JOLLY!

These two neutral-toned living rooms couldn't be more different; one is Nordic rustic chic, the other is traditional (albeit with an untraditionally bold use of pattern). Yet in both, splashes of red signal that the holidays have arrived. And in both, the approach works beautifully.

Eye-catching scarlet wreaths pick up on the year-round pops of red in this Virginia living room. Glass ornaments in a bowl decorate the table.

SIMPLY CHARMING

Two approaches to couldn't-be-easier holiday tabletops: a bunch of pinecones and evergreen branches collected in a bright red bowl, and toy deer ambling through a grove of bottlebrush trees. Merry Christmas!

Pinecones and evergreen branches offer an unfussy alternative to a floral centerpiece.

BRIGHT IDEA! Mirrors installed at the back of glass-fronted cabinets provide a sparkling effect at holiday time—and year-round.

A SONG FOR DECEMBER

Loose sprigs of greenery in sap buckets set the backdrop for a herd of toy deer and a forest of bottle-brush trees. A linen runner unifies the woodland scene.

HUMBLE & HOMEMADE

Less truly is more in this appealing home, where handcrafted is the word at the holidays. Bird ornaments on the tree are cut out of newspaper. The other ornaments are paper labels spritzed with instant coffee (to achieve a perfectly imperfect patina), then stamped with the name of each dinner guest. Greenery wreaths adorn the windows.

This dining room boasts understated holiday décor that somehow still brims with joy.

NATURALLY BEAUTIFUL

When a dining room lives year-round in comfortable neutral shades, bouquets and wreaths of wheat or greenery can usher the room into the season. In both of these rooms, linen table runners provide an elegant but dead-simple anchor for the tabletop decorations.

Wheat—a Swedish Christmas motif—graces the table and the windows in a Connecticut home that is filled with antiques from Scandinavia.

Unadorned greenery punctuated with white taper candles is all that's needed to make this dining room holiday-ready.

3 WAYS TO GET YOUR GREENS

1
Step outside. Grab your clippers and head for any holly, boxwoods, pine, rhododendrons, or other evergreens in your yard. They need pruning anyway, right?

2
Ask the proprietors of your local Christmas tree farm to save fallen branches or leftover sprigs for you.

3
Purchase clippings from your favorite florist.

BRIGHT IDEA! Turn a wreath into a framed work of art by hanging it in front of a mirror.

No red or green in sight—yet is there any doubt that this room is ready for the holidays?

Twas the night
before Christmas
and all through the house
not a creature
was stirring
not even a mouse

EAT

FESTIVE— AND FUN!

It's fine to approach holiday decorating with a sense of playfulness. While the color scheme at left may be one of a kind, it still delivers 100 percent on holiday joy. The whimsical chalkboard on this page bears a heartwarming poem that brings warmth to an otherwise formal room.

The chalkboard is framed in weathered wood that matches the reclaimed elm pedestal table beneath it.

No blossoms allowed in this formal dining room. A bouquet of greenery and an evergreen wreath make a holiday statement.

GREEN SCENE

Flowers are by no means necessary for a holiday table. In these dining rooms, greenery—plus leaves and berries—brings the outdoors inside in a soothing, sophisticated way. White or cream china—whether mismatched or a set—is the perfect complement to this (or almost any) table.

Berries and scarlet leaves provide all the color necessary, and beautifully pair with vintage transferware vases.

Why bother with an elaborate centerpiece when a simple garland creates such a lovely effect?

DRAMATIC—OR DOWN-HOME

Kitchens need Christmas love too. But a little goes a long way in this busy working space. A touch of greenery or a bunch of merry red berries is all it takes to bring the spirit of the season to the room that gives us Christmas cookies and other goodies.

A single evergreen branch suggests a larger tree in this breathtaking all-white kitchen. Greenery is also tucked in atop the surround above the cooktop.

Homey branches of red berries in a tall galvanized tin bucket are the perfect partner to this kitchen's farmhouse-style skirted sink and open shelving filled with colorful vintage dishware.

Perched on the green pine island in this Adirondack-style kitchen is a vintage bottlebrush tree with "snow" inside an oversize antique jar evoking an old-fashioned holiday scene.

Greenery gathered in a vase in the window of this rough-hewn cabin kitchen hints at the holidays to come.

SUBTLE SIGNS OF THE SEASON

Rustic kitchens like these are ready-made for the holidays. A small tree or other touch of green and it all comes into focus.

A potted evergreen would be at home year-round on this concrete kitchen countertop, but in December it takes on the Christmas spirit.

A garland rests lazily above the headboard and gold-framed mirror. Pinecones in a silver bowl and bottlebrush trees add to the Christmas cheer.

A LONG WINTER'S NAP

How could visions of sugarplums not dance in your head when you're sleeping beneath a festive holiday garland? Whether made of evergreen boughs or reminiscent of poinsettias or stars, these gay strands extend the holiday spirit all through the house.

Sleep under the stars! This reclaimed-birch bark garland came from Etsy.

Red-leather garlands in a festive flower shape adorn the windows in this bedroom. A holiday-themed throw on the bed mixes in snowflakes, gingerbread men, and Christmas trees.

BRIGHT IDEA! A box spring encased in a red-striped sheet strikes an unexpected holiday note.

Straw stars shine in the windows above this Gustavian-style headboard.

SWEDISH DREAMS

The pale shades prevalent in Scandinavian style (think white, cream, gray, green) work well with décor made of straw. It's all designed to bring brightness and light to dark winter days.

Birch and willow wreaths are spray-painted gold for a sophisticated effect.

A gold-toned tinsel wreath hangs above a gray-green claw-foot tub in this heavenly pink bath.

BATH & BEYOND

Don't forget to bring the holidays to every corner of your home. Wreaths and greenery warm up even the tiniest bath, and a home office can double as a gift-wrapping station—especially if it's decked out with a merry garland and a small evergreen. Decorated or not, the spirit of the season shines through.

Eucalyptus sprigs say "Happy Holidays" in this tiny powder room.

A banner made of flannel scraps hot-glued to twine and a Christmas tree with a tractor grill tree skirt decorate this home office/ crafts room.

Country, yet contemporary: fluffy ornaments that recall pheasants and feather boas, pinecones lit from within, white porcelain globes, and origami-like poinsettias.

Deck Your Halls: Trees, Garlands, Wreaths & Mantels

There are a few essential building blocks of holiday decorating that can't be overlooked. Chief among them? The tree, indoors or out. Garlands, whether made of traditional evergreen clippings or something else entirely. And, of course, wreaths, the symbol of eternity. And then there's the mantel—a part of the home that seems almost central to the holidays. You can choose to dress up each of these however you like. The only unbreakable rule is that they should reflect what gives you joy.

Getting back to basics: a sweet and simple tabletop tree bedecked with a popcorn garland, red gingham ribbon, and peppermint sticks tied with twine.

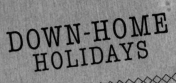

Farmhouses and cabins cry out for trees decorated with old-fashioned charm, but this style is at home almost anywhere. Popcorn garlands and candy canes are time-tested ornaments, and a collection of vintage treasures can be pressed into delightful service.

In this cabin in Franklin, Tennessee, carved wood cookie molds and burlap ribbon adorn the living room tree.

A spruce decorated with
white folk-art-style ornaments
and shiny red balls plays
nicely with candy-striped
wallpaper.

BRIGHT IDEA! Frame fabric in embroidery hoops to create homespun ornaments
with graphic good looks. The tartan plaid is echoed in the ribbons and wrapping below.

{41}

LESS CAN BE MORE

Loading all your ornaments onto an evergreen is in keeping with the abundant spirit of the season, but focusing decorations on a single theme can make an impact. The repetition of the white toy soldiers on this page is striking, and the silver and gold ornaments on the tree opposite result in an appealing glow.

Hobby Lobby toy soldiers, painted white, are a nod to this Connecticut homeowner's British roots. They march in step with shiny green globes.

Silver and gold play starring roles on this Arizona tree!

Against the dark green of the tree, fans and other old-fashioned ornaments of colored glass in soft pastels look as if they've been touched by Jack Frost's wand.

BRIGHT IDEA! Presents wrapped in vintage hat boxes enhance the Victorian theme.

A tabletop tree is festooned with classic ornaments in shades of gold. With this many decorations, even a small tree has a big impact!

VICTORIAN MAGIC

Many of the Christmas traditions we know today originated during the Victorian era, so there's a reason the lavish style of that period seems so right come December. You can stick to a limited color palette of white or gold, work in pastels, or go all-out red for holiday cheer.

This angelic tree dressed in ivory silk roses and silver ornaments was inspired by "The Legend of the Christmas Rose" as told by Selma Lagerlof, the tale of a flower that blooms white blossoms just for December 25.

Very merry indeed! A delightful tree brimming with ornaments, lights, and Santas.

HOMAGE TO THE SEA

Whether you live by the ocean or just appreciate its gifts, a sea-themed tree is a lovely alternative to tradition. You can display actual finds from the beach, as shown here, or take a subtler route with blown-glass ornaments that simply allude to seashells.

Outfit your tree with gifts from the sea. Glue sun-bleached shells, sand dollars, and starfish onto butcher twine for hanging, and be sure to save some to decorate the table.

Dress a Fraser fir in wispy blown-glass shells and other ornaments, and surround the base with gifts wrapped in tissue paper in harmonious hues of violet, pink, and blue.

Reflect the warm glow of your hospitality by bedecking an outdoor tree with blazing lights. Guests will feel welcome before they even turn into the driveway!

TAKE IT OUTSIDE!

Nowhere is it written that you can have only one tree, or that it has to be indoors. Spread the good cheer with a decorated outdoor tree. Natural ornaments are particularly at home outside, but lights are lovely there as well.

No lights required! The striking contrast of white ornaments on an evergreen tree creates a luminosity of its own.

BRIGHT IDEA! Collect sweet gum seedpods, pinecones, and spiraling wisteria pods from your garden, then paint them white with flat interior wall paint (use oil-based paints for pinecones). Voila! A multitude of homemade treasures for your tree!

BASE NOTES

A beautiful tree deserves to be handsome all the way down to the floor. Cover up unsightly tree stands with a lovely tree skirt. Or, be inspired by the alternatives on these pages and use your imagination to come up with a completely original idea!

Ornaments done in white and luminous shades of blue are a lovely reflection of the snow under the bright sky.

A kicky wicker "tree skirt" provides contemporary cover with natural style. Get a similar look by setting your tree inside a basket.

An adorably rustic galvanized tub can hold enough water to nourish your tree for days at a time.

Evergreen garlands from Costco drape the banister in this Washington State home.

SIMPLY STUNNING

Garlands needn't be complicated to bring a festive flourish to a banister. And they can act as a lovely backdrop for more eye-catching decorations, such as the shelves full of books covered in plaid gift wrap below. Store-bought gingerbread houses serve as bookends.

In an upstate New York farmhouse, even the stairway by the back entrance is festooned with a greenery garland.

This intricate garland incorporates fresh asparagus ferns and evergreen shrubs.

PRETTY SPECIAL

In a deliberately spare foyer, a fancy garland has plenty of room to shine—and with the support of just a little extra greenery below, it makes a strong holiday statement.

One garland is good but two are even better! This homeowner twisted together a pinecone garland and one made of mixed greenery and berries to create a one-of-a-kind rope.

SPARKLE AND SHINE

Ramp up the impact of a simple garland by adding a string of lights. While traditional Christmas bulbs are just fine, you can also look for novel ways to get glowing by makers such as Roost or purveyors such as save-on-crafts.com.

The mercury glass globes nestled in this garland are actually a string of lights!

Drape your kitchen windows with garlands of dried apple slices and bunches of cinnamon sticks tied with raffia, and string them under a bower of greens for a lovely combination of fragrances.

Poinsettia blossoms and fir sprigs are woven together in a garland that festoons the doorway.

BRANCH OUT

Greenery is traditional for garlands, but plenty of other materials—fruits, flowers, plants—can be used as well, either to decorate greenery or on their own. Each of the takes here conveys a distinctive spirit: homespun country (far left), old-fashioned floral charm (above left), and Scandinavian (below).

A garland of pine and wheat drapes across the banister of this Connecticut home above a 200-year-old dowry chest from Lapland.

A peg rail in this foyer displays wreaths of varying sizes made of (left to right) pussy willow, faux mountain berry, and frosted pinecones.

MULTIPLE CHOICE

A single wreath is lovely, but when hung in groups of three or more, these circles convey abundance and warmth. Wreaths are particularly versatile—they can be made of greenery, twigs, or myriad other materials, and are equally appropriate outdoors and in.

Lush wreaths created from a thick swirl of multicolored evergreen are adorned with pinecone clusters connected by a thin circle of straw. Grouped together, they make an open front porch even more inviting.

This double-duty wreath is not only beautiful—it also replaces traditional evergreen sprigs with recipe-ready herbs! And it can stay up year-round.

PRIDE OF PLACE

Wreaths that pop up in unexpected spots are particularly delightful. Kitchens, bathrooms, bedrooms—even the back of a door—are all surprising departures from the usual locations.

Half a wreath is far better than none—and just as good as a whole one!—especially when it's adorned with rich reds and russets, densely packed with pinecones on a bed of pine, and balanced with a long leather strip of jingle bells.

NATURAL WONDERS

Wreaths that draw from nature—gardens, meadows, the sea—are especially treasured during winter's dark days. Seashells recall summertime fun at the beach, while brass-plated flowers go the real thing one better: They'll never wilt!

Flowers and leaves are the inspiration for this beautiful brass-plated wreath.

Three starfish nestled in a lush green wreath give a holiday scene a maritime feel.

GO FOR GLAMOUR!

Bright and shiny silver and gold are time-honored alternatives to Christmas red and green, adding a sophisticated touch. Or, look for wreaths made of other light-catching materials, like mother of pearl. Play it straight, or give tradition a lighthearted tilt.

Don't be afraid to have a sense of humor at the holidays. Here, a classical bust goes quirky, crowned by a wreath formed from a gold garland bought at Michaels.

Iridescent mother-of-pearl buttons amplify a room's glow like hundreds of teeny, tiny mirrors—and stand up to off-season storage, no problem.

Rustic meets preppy on this mantel-scape where silver loving cups are filled with evergreen clippings, red ornaments are clustered under a glass cloche, and a tartan plaque and white deer ornament strike a wildlife note.

REINDEER GAMES

Take stock of what you already own and mix it with Christmas staples—ornaments, greenery, stockings—to give your mantel a holiday spin. A red and green, or silver and gold, color scheme seals the deal.

Antique elk antlers draped with ropes of silver and gold balls oversee a rich-looking scene with humble origins: The silver-plate hurricanes come from Costco, the deer figurines hail from Michaels, and the stockings were an Etsy score.

This monochromatic room gets its low-key drama from contrasting textures—a nubby burlap ottoman versus a velvet-covered chair. The Christmas décor follows suit with subtle fir sprigs, wheat stalks, and metal letters spelling peace.

STOCKINGS WERE HUNG

The photographs on these pages prove that stockings have a place in even the most sophisticated of homes. What keeps it upscale? Neutral shades, and the imaginative take on the usual felt or knitted stockings.

BRIGHT IDEA! Antique wooden sock forms stand in for stockings—at least until December 24!

A jingle bell wreath and mercury-glass tree dress up the marble mantel. Burlap stockings hang below.

INTO THE WOODS

Forest motifs and Christmas were made to go together. Snow-covered evergreens, pinecones, and wild creatures congregate to give a mantel rustic warmth.

Linen hand-sewn stockings, bottlebrush trees under a glass cloche, and a hunting trophy achieve the homeowner's wish of wanting this Tennessee cabin to look as if it hadn't changed in a hundred years.

Mason-jar snowglobes, a ceramic owl, and an iron pinecone stocking holder contribute to the sense of a cozy woodland holiday.

A yuletide concept worth its salt: Turn under-a-dollar shakers into mini winter wonderlands by nesting toy evergreens and deer atop iodized "drifts."

Super-Simple Ideas for Homespun Décor

Getting your home into the Christmas spirit doesn't have to mean yet another holiday shopping trip. You can make a Santa's bag full of delightful decorations— including ornaments, tabletop trimmings, even stockings—out of materials you probably already have on hand! Set aside a couple of hours and discover the joys of a handcrafted holiday.

Use what you own: A dash of fake snow and a pair of plastic reindeer transform a year-round display into a wintery scene.

Christmas on the farm: A vintage toy barn gets set for the holidays with coconut-flake snow and mini wreaths.

Thanks to wrapping paper, a ready-made card-stock village becomes a merry town. Tinsel wreaths, tabletop trees, and toy deer complete the tableaux. After the holidays, save the structures and change up the paper next year!

SET THE SCENE

It's easy to create your own little winter fantasyland, either using an item that might be part of your home's year-round décor, or by pressing vintage toys or even card-stock houses into service. All you need is a free tabletop, some fake snow (coconut flakes do the job), miniature evergreens, and adorable animals of your choice.

IT'S ON THE CALENDAR

While traditional advent calendars have cutout windows that open to reveal a picture or perhaps a chocolate, these pouches offer room for a variety of presents. Watch the excitement build as Christmas draws near.

Count down the days to Christmas with little envelopes that hold tiny surprises. Use rubber stamps to ink the dates and other motifs, then embellish by adding tags, string, washi tape, and clip art. Pin the envelopes onto a pretty corkboard.

Off the wall: Take a deconstructed approach to the traditional advent calendar. Simply stamp cotton bags with numbers 1 through 25 and tuck candies, toys, or other treats inside. Let loved ones open one pouch each night.

PEGBOARD
ADVENTURE CALENDAR

Behind each number is a daily idea for getting into the spirit.

STEP
{1}

Draw outline of a tree on a pegboard measuring 24 inches wide by 32 inches high. Mark off outline with painter's tape. Paint tree green.

STEP
{2}

Stitch green yarn through holes of painted tree using a basic backstitch (for a diagram, visit countryliving.com/adcalendar). Knot in back to secure.

STEP
{3}

Use round paper punches to create 25 circles from colored paper.

STEP
{4}

Stamp numbers 1 through 25 on the circles, then jot a holiday activity (such as "mail letter to Santa" or "donate toy to a toy drive") on opposite side.

STEP
{5}

Clip circles to yarn with mini clothespins.

STEP
{6}

Cut 3 stars measuring 3 inches, 3½ inches, and 4 inches from yellow paper. Use adhesive foam to affix stars from largest to smallest, then glue stack to top of tree.

Silver bells: This New York homeowner joined a cluster of jingle bells unearthed at Goodwill with galvanized metal initials from Target. Looped over the knob of the home's front door, they remind guests of the sound of a Christmas sleigh.

COME ON IN!

There's no better place to set a holiday tone than the front door. But don't overlook entryways throughout the house as well. Door knobs provide a built-in anchor for all kinds of whimsical touches.

Pine branches tied together with a simple ribbon decorate a door stripped down to bare wood.

HOLIDAY ROUNDUP

With a little time and effort, you can craft eye-catching wreaths that will last for years to come. Enjoy them on your own walls, or give them as gifts.

TO MAKE this gold-dipped cornhusk wreath, first wrap about 35 husks around an 18-inch diameter straw wreath, using a hot-glue gun to adhere the edges. USE a foam brush to paint the tips of 48 additional corn husks with gold acrylic paint and let dry. STARTING with the outer edge of the wreath, with glue gun, adhere 3 concentric circles of 16 husks each. ATTACH the second ring to the middle of the wreath and the third to its inner edge, as shown.

UPCYCLE toilet paper, paper towel, and mailing tubes into a front door-worthy wreath. USE an X-Acto knife to cut each tube into 2-inch slices. THEN lay a bowl down on a flat surface and arrange the cardboard slices around the bowl, using photo as a guide. HOT-GLUE the slices where their sides meet and perch jingle bells inside.

THIS "LEAF" WREATH is created from bark. TO MAKE, print and cut out the oak- and maple-leaf templates at countryliving.com/birchwreath. TRACE 75 assorted leaves onto twenty-four 6¾-inch-wide by 20½-inch-long sheets of birchbark, and cut out. VARYING the leaf type, hot-glue 30 leaves onto a 20–inch diameter foam wreath form. THEN HOT-GLUE a small wooden cube onto the back of each remaining leaf. USING the photo as a guide, hot-glue the cube-backed leaves atop the original leaves.

CREATE a natural frost ring by hot-gluing acorns, sticks, pinecones, and walnuts to a 16-inch grapevine wreath. APPLY a light coat of white spray-paint for a frosted finish.

Put spools and yarn to a new use! COVER a 16-inch foam wreath in burlap. WRAP various sizes of wooden spools in yarn or felt. WRAP yarn around 5 foam balls. INSERT knitting needles into balls. HOT-GLUE spools and balls to wreath.

TO MAKE this cellophane candy wreath, cut about 30 (1½-inch) sections from cardboard tubes (paper towel rolls, toilet paper rolls, or wrapping paper tubes). ROLL each piece in tissue paper, followed by clear cellophane. CINCH with baker's twine, then trim ends with scallop-edged scissors. GLUE bottom edges of "candy" to a 12-inch embroidery hoop.

START WITH a graphic tea towel to make this paper poinsettia wreath. CUT the tea towel in half lengthwise and wrap pieces around a 16-inch foam wreath, securing with T-pins. CUT 8 slits in sides of 6 red and white cupcake liners; fold corners to form petals. FOLD 12 green liners in half to form leaves. STACK 2 "flower" liners on 2 "leaf" liners; secure to wreath with yellow pins.

HOLIDAY ROUND UP

A birch wood wreath is easy to fabricate. HOT-GLUE 3-inch birch wood coasters side by side to form a wreath shape. ADD a mix of 3-inch and ¾-inch slices atop each joint. FINISH with ribbon for a pop of color.

Christmas cards take on the appearance of art when strung up inside an empty picture frame.

BEST WISHES

What to do with the cards you receive from friends and family each year? A mantel display is just fine, but go one step further with these ideas and really showcase holiday missives.

Twine, clothespins, and nature-themed cards pair up for a charming, low-key display.

All is bright: Jazz up cast-off lightbulbs (these are nightlight bulbs) to make sparkling ornaments. Brush on glittering glue, roll the bulbs in glitter, and let dry for 15 minutes. Then hot-glue a loop of metallic embroidery floss to each bulb's base.

ORNAMENTAL CHARM

Traditional tree baubles can spread cheer throughout the house. Piled high in bowls or inside clear glass hurricane vases, they add a festive touch to coffee tables or other tabletops. The glittery homemade ornaments at left are equally at home dangling from an evergreen branch or doing double-duty elsewhere.

Colorful balls break loose from the tree and help adorn a tabletop overseen by a minimalist white nutcracker.

A silver-toned bowl corrals vintage ornaments for a shimmering, colorful display.

TREE TRIMMERS

Ornaments made from pinecones and woodsy forest scenes pair naturally with a traditional evergreen tree. And if you gather pinecones in your own backyard and hunt for paintings year round at yard sales, these decorations will cost you next to nothing.

BUY bleached pinecones or make your own by submerging pinecones in a solution of 2 parts bleach and 1 part water for 24 hours, then let them dry outside until they open up. (This may take up to a week.) FOR EACH pinecone, cut 1 yard of velvet ribbon into a ¾-yard piece and a ¼-yard piece. HOT-GLUE the end of the longer ribbon to the pinecone base, and tie the shorter ribbon into a bow. TIE the other end of the longer ribbon to a branch of your tree, or to a chandelier.

By the numbers: SCOOP UP amateur artworks at flea markets or yard sales for pennies, then use heavy-duty scissors to cut them into ornaments (for a template, visit countryliving.com/ornament).

TREE TRIMMERS

CRAFT STICK SKIS

PAINT 2 wooden craft sticks. ADJOIN sticks with hot glue, making an X. PAINT 2 toothpicks white. HOT-GLUE metal snaps to one end of each stick. COLOR opposite ends black. HOT-GLUE a ¾-inch piece of twine in a loop to each black end, then glue one pole to the top ski. GLUE second pole at center of first. GLUE twine to ski tops to hang.

RIBBON CANDY

COAT a 24-inch piece of ribbon in fabric stiffener. HANG to dry (about an hour). FOLD ribbon into loops as shown above, adding a dab of hot glue between each layer. GLUE a bead to the top and bottom. ADD an extra dab of glue on the top; affix loop of string to hang.

BUTTON SNOWMAN

GLUE 3 white 2-hole buttons (turn top one perpendicular to create eyes) to white felt; trim felt leaving a 1/8-inch edge. WRAP neck with a piece of rickrack. CUT small hat shape from gray felt and adhere to top with hot glue. GLUE ribbon behind hat to hang.

STRING STARBURSTS

TRACE a 2½-inch circle on a 3-inch birch slice. MARK 8 evenly spaced points around the circle and insert small nails. WRAP embroidery floss around nails, making square and star shapes. ADD a nail to the top; tie on a loop of string to hang.

FABRIC TREE

USE pinking shears to cut 2 triangles measuring 4½ inches high by 2⅜ inches wide from fabric. HOT-GLUE long edges of triangles closed and stuff with batting. INSERT cinnamon stick in opening at the bottom of triangles and glue fabric closed around it. THREAD a loop of string through the top to hang.

FELT DEER HEAD

DOWNLOAD the template at countryliving.com/antlertemplate. TRACE crest portion of the template onto a cork coaster and cut out. TRACE head portion of template onto felt and cut out. REPEAT with cardboard, then trim so it's slightly smaller than the felt. HOT-GLUE felt to cardboard, then glue cardboard to cork crest. PAINT thin sticks white (or leave brown) and hot-glue between the felt and cardboard layers. GLUE a loop of twine at back to hang.

MUSIC SHEET TASSEL

CUT a two-sided page of sheet music featuring a favorite holiday carol into ¼-inch strips. NEXT, GLUE a ¾-inch wooden bead to the end of a wine cork. BEND strips over the bead and cinch around the cork with a rubber band. COVER exposed rubber band with a spare strip. CURL ends of paper around fingertips to fan. LOOP string through strips at top to hang.

PAINTED WALNUT

COAT a walnut with acrylic paint. Once dry, APPLY a layer of clear nail polish for a shiny finish. GLUE a bead to the top and bottom. ADD an extra dab of glue on top; affix loop of string to hang.

SWEATER HOOP

FIT the inner circle of a 3-inch embroidery hoop over the desired section of an old scarf or sweater. CUT out section, leaving a ½-inch edge. FOLD excess fabric over hoop and hot-glue in back. ATTACH outer hoop and thread ribbon through hardware at top to hang.

To give a basic linen napkin a holiday glow, dip a corncob in gold fabric paint, then roll it across the napkin. Let it dry, and follow the paint manufacturer's instructions to heat-set the paint so that the napkin can be washed and used again.

BRIGHT IDEA! Freshen up a simple Kraft paper tag with a sprig of rosemary tied on with twine.

Help guests keep up with their drinks by wrapping each glass stem in a different color of embroidery floss. Use mini Glue Dots to secure thread at the base of the stem and along the way as you wrap the thread up, and back down.

Cover artificial pomegranates with copper leaf for festive décor that will never spoil.

TABLETOP DELIGHTS

A little bit of homespun ingenuity brings individuality to your holiday dinner or party. Gold tones are particularly festive, but reds, greens, and blues also make the season bright.

Simple gift tags costing less than a dollar each take center stage when hung in vintage bird cages. The paper doves also look lovely dangling from chandeliers or doorknobs.

Leave the popcorn behind and fashion a garland from coffee filters! STACK 12 ruffled coffee filters, randomly mixing white and natural-colored ones, and staple the center. REPEAT. Twenty stacks will yield a 10-foot garland. POKE a hole near the center of each stack with a small nail, then cut a piece of twine at least a foot longer than the desired length of your garland and knot one end. THREAD on one stack and secure by knotting the twine on the other side, then tie another knot 6 inches down. SLIDE on a second stack until it presses against the last knot, and continue until all stacks are strung. CRUNCH the filters with your fingers to transform each stack into a pom-pom.

PART TWO

Wonderful Gifts to Make

A present created by hand deserves the most beautiful of wrappings.

PICTURE-PERFECT PILLOWS

SCAN and upload a photo, then place it in an 8½-inch by 11-inch Microsoft Word document, leaving a ½-inch border. PRINT onto an ink-jet fabric sheet, and cut a same-size piece of backing fabric. PIN the 2 pieces together, right sides facing, and stitch, leaving a 4-inch-wide opening. TURN right side out, stuff with loose fiberfill stuffing, and blind stitch the opening closed.

Handmade Gifts from the Heart

Whether you're aiming for a 100 percent hand-crafted holiday this year or just want to create a present for someone special, you'll find the ideal item on the pages that follow. Nothing says "I love you" like a one-of-a kind object invested with time and talent. It's something money can't buy!

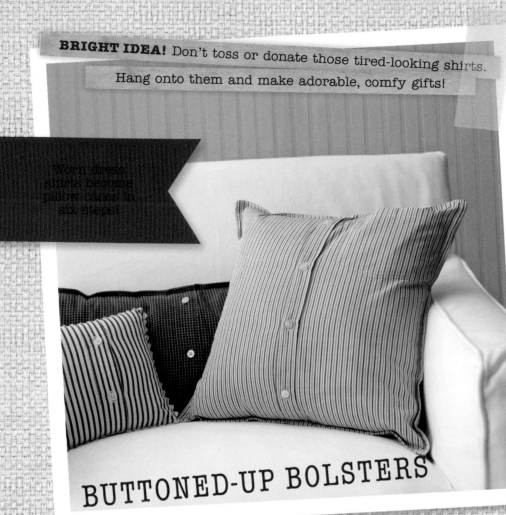

BRIGHT IDEA! Don't toss or donate those tired-looking shirts. Hang onto them and make adorable, comfy gifts!

Worn dress shirts become pillow cases in six steps!

BUTTONED-UP BOLSTERS

STEP 1: Iron shirt to smooth out wrinkles. Button it, then pin the shirt's front and back to each other to keep them together when cutting.

STEP 2: Cut out the shirt to match the shape of your pillow insert—adding 2 inches to both the width and length, and centering the row of buttons down the front. (You'll now have two pieces of fabric.)

STEP 3: Repin the fabric so the shirt's finished sides face each other. Sew the pieces together using a 6/8-inch seam. Snip the corners at an angle to ease turning.

STEP 4: Unbutton the fabric and turn the pillowcase right side out. Iron, then rebutton.

STEP 5: Topstitch around the case twice—first 1/8 inch from the edge, then 3/8 inch from the edge—to finish it.

STEP 6: Unbutton the case, insert the pillow, then rebutton and fluff.

CUSTOMIZED CUSHION

Transform a basic round pillow into a treasured possession. FIRST, purchase a 15-inch diameter pillow case and a pillow insert. CENTER a 12-inch dinner plate facedown on the empty pillow case; using a pencil, trace the shape. Within that circle, repeat with a 9-inch salad plate. USING a ruler and chalk, divide and mark the inner circle into equal quarters. WITHIN each quarter, center a 2½-inch diameter juice glass; using a pencil, trace the shape. TRACE over all six pencil-marked circles with a red, chisel-tip fabric marker. LET DRY for 2 minutes, then slide the pillow insert inside the case. RUN a long needle threaded with embroidery floss through the center of each of the 4 small circles twice, to create tufting. SECURELY knot the floss on the pillow's back side; clip excess and dust off chalk marks.

Turn a basic pillow into one that's button-cute!

PRIZED PILLOWS!

KNIT WITS!

A beloved sweater gets new life as a fuzzy pillow sham.

SWEATER PILLOW SHAM

YOU'LL NEED an 18-inch square pillow insert and a large sweater, cut into two 19-inch squares. SEW the right sides of the wool together along the edges, leaving the bottom open. TURN the right side out and insert the pillow form, then blind stitch the bottom closed. FOR THE FLOWER, cover a 2-inch circle of card stock with a piece of thin sweater; hot-glue to the circle's back. NEXT, fold a 3- by 20-inch strip of another sweater in half lengthwise. HOT-GLUE the edges together, then sew a running stitch down the length along the glued seam. ONCE you've stitched the entire length, pull the thread to gather the fabric and knot. HOT-GLUE the gathered edge into a circle to the back of the card stock, then hot-glue a pin-back in the center and affix to the pillow.

MESSAGE
GLOVES

Start with any
knit gloves.

STEP 1: Slide one
glove onto your
hand. Using a
pastel chalk pencil,
mark each knuckle
with a horizontal
line at the bottom
of each finger (the
first joint) and
another just below
the second joint.
Remove the glove,

then repeat for
the other hand.
If needed, enlist
a friend to mark
your dominant
hand.

STEP 2: Lay the
gloves, marked
sides up, on a
flat surface.
Working within the
horizontal lines,
and using the chalk
pencil, spell out the

phrase you plan to
stitch across both
gloves. Try the
gloves on to check
that your letters
are positioned to
your satisfaction.

STEP 3: Using
6-strand
embroidery thread
that contrasts
with the color of
your gloves, sew
directly over the

chalk letters with
a basic stem stitch,
making sure to sew
through the top
layer only. (For a
quick stem-stitch
tutorial, check out
countryliving.com
/stemstitch.)
Remove any stray
chalk with a damp
cotton swab.

Bless your heart.

There, there.

Keep your nose clean.

DAINTY HANDKERCHIEFS
(WITH DRY HUMOR)

START with three 12-inch square cotton hankies. FOR EACH, handwrite the phrase of your choice in the bottom-right corner with a water-soluble marker. THEN embroider over the letters using a standard stem stitch. REMOVE any stray marks with a dab of water.

KITTED OUT

Instead of a single present, delight loved ones with a customized kit packed with stuff they're sure to use—buttons, threads, and needles for a friend who likes to sew; polishes, brushes, and buffing cloths for a well-dressed dad; or cookie cutters, sprinkles, and icing tubes for a friend who bakes. TO CREATE these kits, start by spraying a clean tin (we used old metal cookie containers) with Rust-Oleum Universal All-Surface paint in white; let dry. NEXT, download an image to match the tin's contents at countryliving. com/dec-templates. PRINT the silhouette and cut out, then spray the back with adhesive. USING a pair of craft tweezers, pick up the graphic and place it, right side up, on the tin's lid. ONCE IT DRIES, coat the lid and base with a spray sealer and let dry. USE black card stock, cut to the tin's dimensions, to create dividers, if desired. Then fill with your goodies.

Fabric scraps pair with heart-shaped cookie cutters for pincushions with homey charm.

COOKIE CUTTER PIN CUSHIONS

STEP 1: To construct the base of each pincushion, place the sharp side of a heart-shaped cookie cutter atop a thin piece of Styrofoam (such as a produce tray from a grocery store). Press the cutter down to imprint the Styrofoam, then cut out the heart shape.

STEP 2: Cut a heart-shaped piece of fabric that's about ½ inch larger, all the way around, than the Styrofoam shape. Lay the fabric, right side down, on a flat surface and cover the back with Aleene's Tacky Glue, then press the Styrofoam against the fabric. Pull the excess fabric up around the Styrofoam's edges and secure with more glue; let dry for 30 minutes.

STEP 3: Meanwhile, cut a square of fabric that's at least three inches larger, all the way around, than the cookie cutter. Hold the cutter, sharp side up, on your lap and lay the fabric right side down over the cutter. Push fiberfill stuffing into the cutter until the fabric protrudes about ¾ inch past the cutter, forming the pincushion. To close the cushion, fold over the remaining fabric and secure with a running stitch.

STEP 4: With the cushion still inside the cutter, cover the cushion's bottom with a generous coat of glue. Push the Styrofoam into the cutter so that it presses against the glue; hold in place for 3 minutes. Let dry for 30 minutes.

This bracelet's as neat as a pin!

GOLDEN SAFETY PIN BRACELET

Golden safety pins come together to form surprisingly posh arm candy. SIMPLY LINK ten ¾-inch-long pins into a chain, and repeat to assemble 11 chains total. THEN, use 2 gold-tone jump rings to connect all of the chains: With needle-nose pliers, open 1 jump ring, thread it through the coil of the last pin in each chain, and close the ring. REPEAT with a jump ring on the other end of the chains, then slide on a gold-tone swiveling lobster clasp before closing the ring.

THIMBLE NECKLACE

Look for inexpensive vintage thimbles at flea markets or on Etsy—you can usually score one for less than $5. USE a small hammer and a two-penny nail to punch a tiny hole in the center of the thimble's top. INSERT a flat-head pin through the hole from the inside, so the pin's head remains inside the thimble. TWIST the pin's exposed wire into a closed loop with needle-nose pliers, then use the pliers to attach a 6-mm jump ring to the loop. THREAD the pendant onto a chain necklace.

A humble thimble shines up nicely as a necklace.

FROM FOUND OBJECTS TO FINE JEWELS

CHANDELIER PRISM PENDANT

USE pliers to remove any existing wiring. THEN tightly wrap 22-gauge gold craft wire around the top of the prism, as pictured. FORM a wire loop for your necklace chain; then, using pliers, cut the wire 2 inches past the loop before securing its end inside the wrapped wire. STRING a length of gold-plated chain through the wire loop. ATTACH a gold S-hook to each end of the chain. For a fanciful finish, present the necklace inside a velvet pouch.

A cast off chandelier prism becomes a stunning necklace—fast!

CUSTOM JEWEL BOX

Start with a plain craft-store box.

STEP 1: Sand the outside and inside of your box with fine-grade sandpaper; wipe clean, then use a pencil to lightly sketch a name on the box's top. Trace over the first letter with a glue pen. Immediately cover the letter with a thin leather cord, cutting or connecting the cord to the next letter as you go. Continue this process until the entire name is covered. Let dry for 30 minutes.

STEP 2: Spray the entire box with 2 coats of white matte paint, allowing at least 30 minutes of drying time after each coat.

STEP 3: Measure the inside width and depth of the box's bottom. Cut a piece of felt to 1 yard long and a width slightly narrower than that of the box. Next, accordion-fold the felt: Beginning at one of the felt piece's shorter ends, make a fold that's slightly shorter than the depth of the box; secure with a thin line of hot glue. Carefully fold the felt back the other way and glue in place to complete one accordion fold. Repeat for the entire felt piece.

STEP 4: Insert the folded felt into the box; trim any excess material. Secure the felt to each upper and lower inside corner of the box with hot glue. Let dry again before presenting it as a gift.

PRETTY, PLEASE

RED LEATHER BOW

STEP 1: Download, print, and cut out the bracelet template at countryliving.com /bowbracelet. Use the template to cut out a large, oblong piece of leather as well as a thin center band.

STEP 2: Wrap the thin band around the center of the larger piece to form the bow's middle, using the photo below for guidance. Secure the band on the bow's wrong side with hot glue. Let dry for 5 minutes.

STEP 3: Lay the bow on a flat surface, wrong side up. Following the package instructions in a snap-fastener kit, make the bracelet adjustable by attaching 2 snap studs on one end, centering and spacing them about ½ inch apart; repeat on the other end with snap sockets.

Shape some snappy arm candy!

HEAD-TURNING HEADBANDS

JAZZ up inexpensive fabric headbands in just minutes
by hot-gluing on adornments. CHECK OUT the selection
at mjtrim.com, such as the vibrant straw flower and
braided frog closure above. LET the glue dry, about
3 minutes, then present your crowning achievement
as a glamorous gift.

KITCHEN CHARM

Starting with plain ceramic dishes, freehand the tea bag, tag, and spoon designs, using this image as a guide, with Pebeo's Porcelaine fine point marker. Don't worry if you make a mistake—the ink can be washed off for up to 72 hours. Allow at least 24 hours' drying time, then bake the items for 35 minutes in a 300°F oven. Let cool completely and wash (the ink's dishwasher-safe) before giving.

WITTY TEA SET

Give afternoon tea a tromp l'oeil twist.

PAINTED KNIFE BLOCK

All it takes to elevate a
basic knife block is a pencil
and some paint. BEGIN by
spray-painting the block
with 2 coats of Rust-
Oleum's white semigloss.
ALLOW 2 hours of drying
time between coats; then
let dry overnight.
NEXT, lay the block faceup.
Using a set of 4 knives,
lay one utensil atop the
block in a spot that reflects
the blade's placement when
stored; carefully trace
the shape with a pencil.
REPEAT with the other
3 knives. Fill the inside of
each shape with another
paint color. LET DRY for
2 hours, add a second coat,
then let dry again before
giving.

RECIPE ORGANIZER

A flea-market spoon is
the secret ingredient
to punching up an
unfinished box.

STEP 1: With a foam
brush, stain the box,
inside and out, with
Minwax Wood finish in
Classic Gray. Let dry
overnight.

STEP 2: Using your
hands, bend a teaspoon

at a 90-degree angle.
Lightly sand the widest
point of the handle's
back side.

STEP 3: Apply Glass,
Metal & More glue
along the sanded area.
Center the spoon atop
the box, press and hold
for 1 minute, then let
set overnight.

CUTTING BOARD TABLET HOLDER

WITH wood glue, adhere a Scrabble tile holder to the bottom center of an 8½-inch-wide by 16-inch-long cutting board. LET DRY for 2 hours. NEXT, use wood glue to affix a 9-inch-long wooden doorstop to the bottom center of the board's opposite side as shown. LET DRY for 2 hours. FINALLY, paint the entire piece with acrylic latex paint and let dry overnight. BUFF the edges lightly with sandpaper to achieve a weathered look.

Who doesn't want a little kitchen tech support?

GET COOKING!

"EMBROIDERED" KITCHEN CANISTERS

RICE

FLOUR

SUGAR

Cross-stitch makes the leap from fabric to glassware with help from a free font and transparent sticker sheets. GO to myfonts.com and download the Home Sweet Home font. USE IT to type out the names of pantry staples, adding a decorative flourish if you like, in a Microsoft Word document, then adjust the type size and alignment to fit your canisters. FOLLOWING package instructions from the decal sheets, print your document(s). ONCE the ink has dried, lightly coat each sheet with a thin layer of hairspray, to prevent smearing; let dry. CUT OUT and trim each label, then affix to the canisters. NOTE: The labels won't be entirely waterproof, so let the recipient know to wash them carefully by hand when necessary.

TERRIFIC TABLE TOPPERS

PULL a sweater sleeve over a bowl, lining up the finished cuff with the top rim, and hot-glue. THEN trim the wool so it reaches the bowl's bottom edge and hot-glue in place.

"SWEATER" DISHES

BRIGHT IDEA! You can create these candleholders for barely $2 a pop!

DRESSED-UP VOTIVES

The trick to transforming plain glass votive holders? Humble upholstery webbing. SIMPLY CUT a piece of webbing to the same length as the holder's circumference, then trim the webbing a tad bit shorter than the holder's height. COAT the webbing's raw edges with Mod Podge to prevent fraying; let dry for 20 minutes. NEXT, affix the webbing around the holder with thin lines of hot glue and let dry for 5 minutes. Package a few of these beauties together with scented candles inside and cross someone off your list.

Decorative dishes kept in stitches deserve a warm welcome in winter.

GOLDEN BOWLS

Upcycle shredded paper into a set of gilded decorative bowls. First, choose a bowl (or multiple different-size bowls) to use as a mold. For each container you plan to create, follow these steps:

STEP 1: Tightly cover the outside of your bowl with plastic wrap, securing it on the inside with painter's tape, and turn upside down. In another bowl, mix equal parts Elmer's white school glue and water. Dip shredded paper into the mixture, evenly coating each piece. Next, lay the strips atop the plastic-wrapped bowl so they overlap, until the bowl's exterior is completely covered. Let dry for 3 hours.

STEP 2: Flip the bowl right side up and trim away any excess paper along the rim with scissors. Then, loosen and separate your paper bowl from the plastic-wrapped bowl.

STEP 3: Paint the interior of your bowl with white acrylic paint and let it dry for 1 hour; then paint the exterior and let it dry for an hour.

STEP 4: Cover the outside of your paper bowl with wax paper, securing it to the bowl's outer rim with painter's tape. Next, apply gold leaf to the bowl's interior using a gilding kit. Follow the package instructions, and let set overnight.

STEP 5: Apply neutral-toned Liberon Wax to the interior of the bowl with a soft cloth. Allow the wax to set for an hour, then gently buff to a shine with a clean soft cloth. Finally, remove the tape and wax paper, and present your lustrous treasures.

Bowled over! Papier-mâché is the secret to this fancy set.

FOR THE BIRD-LOVERS

BRIGHT IDEA! Enclose each oval soap in a coffee filter before boxing—the ruffles gather neatly around curves.

SOAPS THAT RAISE THE BAR

Homemade soaps wrapped in beautiful papers copied from a vintage bird guide please on every level.

A goat's-milk formula and a beguiling bird mold—along with thoughtful packaging—result in bars that seem like they cost a fortune. FIRST, melt the soap according to package instructions (for soap-making base, try bumbleberry.com). POUR the mixture into a silicone mold. LET IT set for 4 hours, then pop out your bar. TO WRAP the soaps, use unbleached coffee filters, rectangular cardboard boxes, and paper color-copied from a vintage bird guide.

AVIAN MOUSEPAD

DOWNLOAD free illustrations of your choice from graphicsfairy.com. RESIZE the image to 10-inch-wide by 7¼-inch-high and print onto fabric-transfer paper. CUT OUT the image from the transfer paper, remove the backing, and place, right side facing up, on the smooth side of a piece of top-grain leather. IRON the image onto the leather, following the transfer-paper package instructions, and trim away the excess leather bordering the image.

Put a bird
on it!
(Or seven.)

This firewood carrier costs less than $15 to make!

CANVAS FIREWOOD CARRIER

A plain canvas tote bag is the secret to this craft.

STEP 1: Turn a canvas bag inside out, then use a seam ripper to undo the gusseted corners. Using scissors, cut the bag along the side seams so that it lays completely flat when open.

STEP 2: Lay the bag wrong side up. Using a pencil and a ruler, draw an 8½-inch diagonal line across each of the bag's corners. Cut the bag along the lines, as shown; discard corner pieces. Then fold each cut edge over by ¼ inch and topstitch in place.

STEP 3: Cut a piece of faux bois oilcloth that measures 18¼ inches long by 13½ inches wide. Flip the bag right side up, then lay the panel across the bag's middle section, as shown. Using bright-orange thread, topstitch the panel in place along its edges.

STEP 4: Reinforce the handles by folding each strap back on itself, as shown. Clamp or pin the strap in place, then stitch it together. Repeat for the second strap.

You can sew this handsome iPod case for a song!

WILD STYLE

BRIGHT IDEA! If you want to craft a case for a different device, visit countryliving.com/leathercase to learn how to make templates.

WOODLAND IPOD CASE

Scan your own photos or use the woodland imagery shown, which was cribbed from a vintage postcard.

STEP 1: Download the templates for the case's front and back, sized to fit an iPod Touch, at countryliving.com /leathercase. If using the woodland image featured on the templates, print each template onto a transfer sheet and cut out, then skip to Step 3. Otherwise, print each template onto a piece of regular paper and cut out.

STEP 2: If using your own images, resize them, if necessary, to fit the templates. Then print each image onto a transfer sheet. Place the template for the case's front atop one image; trace and cut out. Repeat for the back with the other template and image.

STEP 3: Following the package instructions for the transfer sheets, iron each image onto the smooth side of a leather scrap that's at least 3 inches wide by 5 inches long. Cut the leather to the exact shapes of the images.

STEP 4: Using a sewing machine, and with the photo above as a guide, stitch a decorative seam along the top of the front and back pieces, leaving a $3/16$-inch edge. Align the pieces, right sides facing out, with a $1/16$-inch seam allowance, leaving the top of the pouch open. To end on a high note, pair it with a new set of earbuds.

PRETTY PAPERS

A journal and two matching watch straps are the ingredients for a secret diary.

BUCKLED-UP JOURNAL

STEP 1: Measure and mark 2 spots inside the front cover of the notebook; one, 2 inches from the top; the other, 2 inches from the bottom; both, 1½ inches from the spine. Next, measure and mark 2 spots inside the back cover; one, 2 inches from the top;

the other, 2 inches from the bottom; both, 5½ inches from the spine. Using a hammer and a four-penny nail, punch holes through all 4 marks.

STEP 2: For each of the 4 watchband pieces, measure and mark a spot ⅛ inch from the end

that would attach to a watch. Use the hammer and nail to punch through all 4 marks.

STEP 3: Place one buckle-end watchband piece atop the front cover, aligning the punched holes. Push one ⁵⁄₁₆-inch-wide by ⁵⁄₁₆-inch-

long brass rivet through both holes; set according to package instructions. Repeat for the other hole and buckle-end watchband piece. Then flip the notebook over and repeat for the remaining hole and watchband pieces.

CHRISTMAS-TREE CARDS

A sweet alternative to store-bought cards, these greetings put your tree-decorating skills to work on a small scale. FOLD a piece of 8½-inch by 11-inch card stock in half lengthwise and crease. FREEHAND a Christmas tree onto the front of the card. FOR the card below left, attach small bugle beads and paillettes to the tree (use craft glue for all designs). TO REPLICATE the middle version, cut out ornaments (made by tracing a button), a tree base, and a star from patterned fabric and adhere. MAKE the last card by zigzagging a length of ribbon across the tree. FOLD the ends under and glue, then try other widths of ribbon to craft a base, star, and gift. OR USE your imagination, and whatever supplies you have on hand, to make your own one-of-a-kind cards.

CUSTOMIZED NOTEPAD

STEP 1: Select one or more photos and use a program like Photoshop to silhouette and size each image so that it measures about 2½ inches high. If desired, apply a filter to achieve a colorful tint, like the red one above. Place one image in the bottom right corner of a horizontal Microsoft Word document. To create 2 notepad a per sheet, align a duplicate of that image (or use a different one) along the bottom edge of the document, just left of center, according to your on-screen ruler. (Repeat on separate pages, as desired.)

STEP 2: Print out enough 8½-inch-wide by 11-inch-long sheets (at least 20) to make a pad; stack, then cut in half. To form a backing for the pad, cut out an 8½-inch-wide by 5½-inch-long piece of cardboard.

STEP 3: Stack and align the pages with the cardboard piece at the bottom. Clamp the stack together on the left and right sides, near the top, with binder clips.

STEP 4: Using a paintbrush, apply a thin layer of Aleene's Tacky Glue across the top of the notepad, making sure to completely cover both the paper and cardboard backing. Let dry for two hours before adding a second layer. Let dry again, then remove clamps before using.

A Basic Sugar-Cookie Dough can be rolled out and cut into shapes, formed into slice-and-bake logs or pushed through a cookie press yielding a wide variety of treats. See p. 130 for the recipe.

Homemade Gifts from the Kitchen

Christmas presents don't come any sweeter than the mouthwatering morsels you whip up yourself. Cookies and candies—even breads, crackers, special nuts, and seasonings—are all thoughtful, delicious expressions of affection. And when they're packaged in adorable boxes, bottles, bags, and tins, the whole presentation is irresistible. Happy gifting!

BASIC SUGAR-COOKIE DOUGH

Working time 10 min. *Total time* 10 min.

1 stick unsalted butter, softened
1½ cups confectioners' sugar
2 large eggs
1 teaspoon vanilla extract
¼ teaspoon salt
2½ cups all-purpose flour

In a large bowl, beat together butter and confectioners' sugar using an electric mixer set on medium-high speed. Add eggs, vanilla, and salt and beat until combined. Reduce mixer speed to low, add flour, and mix until dough is smooth. (**NOTE**: Basic Sugar-Cookie Dough can be refrigerated for up to 5 days or frozen for up to 3 months; thaw in refrigerator before using.)

VARIATIONS

Linzer Tart Christmas Trees

Makes About 20 cookies *Working time* 35 min. *Total time* 1 hr. 30 min., plus chilling

  Basic Sugar-Cookie Dough
  (recipe above)
2 cups slivered almonds, finely ground
½ cup raspberry or red currant preserves
  Confectioners' sugar

1. When making Basic Sugar-Cookie Dough, beat almonds into butter and confectioners' sugar at beginning of recipe. Shape dough into a disk and wrap tightly in plastic wrap. Chill until firm, about 4 hours.
2. Preheat oven to 350°F. Roll dough to ¼-inch thickness and cut out Christmas tree shapes using 4-inch cutters. For half of tree cookies, use a 2 ½-inch Christmas tree cutter to stamp out a second tree in the center of dough. (Only tree outline will be used; if desired, you can bake smaller inner trees later.)
3. Bake on parchment-lined baking sheets until firm and lightly browned, 10 to 12 minutes. Let cookies cool on pan for 2 minutes. Transfer to a wire rack and let cool. Spread preserves atop solid-tree cookies. Dust tree-outline cookies with confectioners' sugar and carefully place atop solid cookies. Fill cut-out windows with more preserves, if desired, and let preserves set, 30 to 60 minutes.

Cranberry, Pistachio, and Chocolate-Chunk Cookies

Makes About 36 cookies *Working time* 25 min. *Total time* 35 min., plus chilling

  Basic Sugar-Cookie Dough
  (recipe above left)
¾ cup dried cranberries
¾ cup chopped pistachios
6 ounces milk chocolate, chopped

1. Mix Basic Sugar-Cookie Dough and remaining ingredients. Divide into three 2-inch logs and wrap tightly in plastic wrap. Chill until firm, about 4 hours.
2. Preheat oven to 350°F. Slice logs into ¼-inch-thick cookies and bake on parchment-lined baking sheets until firm and lightly browned, 8 to 10 minutes. Transfer to a wire wrack and let cool.

Red-and-White Marbled Cookies

Makes About 36 cookies. *Working time* 30 min. *Total time* 40 min., plus chilling

  Basic Sugar-Cookie Dough
  (recipe above left)
  Red food coloring
  Coarse white sanding sugar

1. Divide the Basic Sugar-Cookie Dough in half. On a cutting board, tint one half red by kneading in red food coloring, adding 1 drop at a time until desired color is achieved.
2. Roll each half into a 1¼-inch-thick rope. Lay both pieces side by side on cutting board and cross red over white, then white over red until 1 larger, twisted log is formed. Gently knead to smooth out twist and incorporate colors for a marbled effect. Wrap tightly in plastic wrap and chill until firm, about 4 hours.
3. Preheat oven to 350°F. Roll dough in sanding sugar. Slice into ¼-inch-thick cookies. Bake on parchment-lined baking sheets until firm and lightly browned, 8 to 10 minutes. Transfer to a wire rack and let cool.

Pressed Flower Cookies

Makes About 50 cookies *Working time* 25 min. *Total time* 35 min.

  Basic Sugar-Cookie Dough
  (recipe at left)
  Silver dragées

1. Preheat oven to 350°F. Load Basic Sugar-Cookie Dough into a cookie press fitted with a flower stencil. Press, according to manufacturer's instructions, onto baking sheets. Repeat with remaining dough. Decorate center of cookies with silver dragées.
2. Bake until cookies are firm and lightly browned, about 8 minutes. Let cookies cool on pan for 2 minutes. Transfer to a wire rack and let cool.

Chocolate-Filled Stars

Makes About 24 cookies *Working time* 35 min. *Total time* 1 hr. 10 min., plus chilling

  Basic Sugar-Cookie Dough
  (recipe above left)
⅔ cup semisweet or milk chocolate chips
¼ cup heavy cream
⅔ cup confectioners' sugar

1. Divide Basic Sugar-Cookie Dough in half. Pat each portion into a disk and wrap tightly in plastic wrap. Chill until firm, about 4 hours.
2. Preheat oven to 350°F. Roll dough to ¼-inch thickness and cut out star shapes using a 3-inch cutter. Bake cookies on parchment-lined baking sheets until firm and lightly browned, 8 to 10 minutes. Transfer to a wire rack and let cool.
3. To make filling: Place chocolate chips in a small heatproof bowl. In a small saucepan, bring cream to a boil. Pour cream over chocolate and stir until smooth. Let cool to room temperature and stir in confectioners' sugar until combined and mixture reaches a thick frosting consistency. Spread chocolate filling on cookie, then top with another cookie. Repeat with remaining cookies.

All five of these charming cookies start with just one recipe!

Linzer Tart Christmas Trees

Cranberry, Pistachio, and Chocolate-Chunk Cookies

Red-and-White Marbled Cookies

Pressed Flower Cookies

Chocolate-Filled Stars

{131}

BRIGHT IDEA! Gather a stack of cookies together by threading ribbon through the buttonholes, and present the cookies in a perfectly sized papier-mâché box with a snowflake stenciled on the lid.

These buttery delights are cute as, well, you know.

SUGAR-COOKIE BUTTONS

Makes 4 boxes of 6 cookies *Working time* 55 min. *Total time* 1 hr. 30 min., plus chilling

- 2 sticks unsalted butter, at room temperature
- 1 cup sugar
- 2 eggs
- 2 teaspoons vanilla
- 3⅓ cups all-purpose flour, plus more for parchment and cutters
- ½ teaspoon salt

1. In a large bowl, using an electric mixer on high, beat butter and sugar together until light and fluffy. Reduce mixer to medium, and beat in eggs, 1 at a time. Beat in vanilla. Reduce mixer to low, and beat in flour and salt until soft dough forms. Divide dough into 4 equal pieces and pat each into a disk. Wrap each disk tightly with plastic wrap and refrigerate overnight.

2. Roll out each disk between 2 sheets of well-floured parchment to ⅛-inch thickness. Transfer to a baking pan, wrap tightly with plastic wrap, and refrigerate, 30 to 60 minutes.

3. Remove and unwrap 2 dough disks. Use a well-floured 3-inch round cutter to cut out 12 cookies. Transfer to a parchment-lined baking sheet, spacing cookies about 1 inch apart. To make each resemble a button: Using the blunt side of a 2¼-inch round cutter, indent a circle on the cookie's surface. Then, using a straw, poke 2 holes near the center of each cookie. Repeat with 2 remaining dough disks.

4. Preheat oven to 400°F. Meanwhile, refrigerate pans with cookies until chilled, about 15 minutes. Bake until cookies are golden around edges and firm, about 5 minutes. (If necessary, use a skewer to reopen buttonholes.) Transfer to a wire rack to cool.

5. To package, string a ribbon through a stack of 6 button cookies and tie before placing in box. Repeat with remaining cookies to fill 3 more boxes.

These cookies look like adorable tiny individual pies.

BRIGHT IDEA! To package, insert a 4-inch-diameter paper doily and 2 cookies in each of five 4⅜-inch-wide by 1-inch-high by 4⅜-inch-deep boxes. Stack the boxes and secure with baker's twine.

CINNAMON-SUGAR LATTICE COOKIES

Makes 2 gifts of 10 cookies each (20 cookies total) **Working time** *1 hr. 25 min.* **Total time** *2 hr. 10 min., plus chilling*

7½	cups all-purpose flour, plus more for dusting parchment
3	teaspoons ground cinnamon
1½	teaspoons ground nutmeg
1½	teaspoons baking powder
¾	teaspoon fine salt
3	large eggs
4½	sticks butter (2½ cups each), at room temperature
2¼	cups granulated sugar
2¼	teaspoons vanilla extract
¼	cup white sanding sugar

1. In a large bowl, combine the first 5 ingredients; set aside. In a medium bowl, beat eggs and set aside.

2. In a large mixing bowl, using an electric mixer on medium-high speed, beat butter until light and fluffy. Beat in granulated sugar, then vanilla and egg mixture. Reduce mixer speed to low and gradually beat in reserved flour mixture just until the dough comes together. Remove the dough from the bowl and divide into 4 equal pieces. Shape into disks, wrap tightly in plastic wrap, and refrigerate for at least 2 hours or up to 3 days.

3. Remove dough from refrigerator and unwrap. Place each disk between lightly floured pieces of parchment, dusting with more flour to keep dough from sticking, and roll out each to a 14-inch square that's ⅛ inch thick. Stack dough squares with parchment on a baking sheet, cover sheet tightly with plastic wrap, and refrigerate for 30 minutes.

4. Preheat oven to 350°F. Meanwhile, remove baking sheet from refrigerator and unwrap. Remove 2 dough squares. Rewrap baking sheet and return to refrigerator. Unwrap 1 dough square. Using a pizza cutter, slice the square into ½-inch-wide strips. Repeat with the second dough square. Then, working with the first dough square, gently fold back every other strip in half, taking care not to create a crease at the bend. Position one strip of dough from the second square perpendicularly against the bends in the strips you just folded back. Unfold the bent strips so that they lie atop the perpendicular strip. Repeat this crisscrossing process (folding back the strips in the first square that are now covered by the perpendicular strip, placing another strip from the second square perpendicularly against those bends, and unfolding the bent strips so they lie atop the new perpendicular strip) until a lattice pattern is woven through half of the dough square. Turn the parchment 180 degrees and repeat the process. Line 2 baking sheets with parchment. Using a 3½-inch round cutter, cut out cookies and transfer to prepared baking sheets. (Gather scraps, wrap tightly in plastic wrap and refrigerate.) Sprinkle cookies lightly with sanding sugar. Bake until golden around the edges and firm, 11 to 14 minutes. Cool cookies on baking sheets for 5 minutes, then transfer to a wire rack to cool completely. Repeat with the 2 remaining dough squares.

5. Remove gathered scraps from refrigerator, form into a disk, and chill until firm, at least 30 minutes. Then repeat steps for rolling, chilling, lattice-making, baking, and cooling to create the last few cookies.

SHORTBREAD COOKIES

Makes 4 boxes of 24 cookies (6 of each glaze)
Working time 1 hr. 45 min. *Total time* 2 hr. 45 min.,
plus chilling

4   sticks unsalted butter, at room
    temperature
2   cups confectioners' sugar
4   teaspoons vanilla
5   cups all-purpose flour
1   teaspoon salt
    Glaze (recipes below)

1. In a large bowl, using an electric mixer on medium-high speed, beat butter until smooth, about 8 minutes. Add sugar and beat until light and fluffy. Beat in vanilla. Reduce mixer to low, add flour and salt, and beat until combined.
2. Divide dough into 4 equal pieces and pat each into a square. Roll out each square between 2 sheets of lightly floured parchment to ¼-inch thickness. Transfer to a baking pan, wrap tightly with plastic wrap, and refrigerate, about 2 hours.

3. Preheat oven to 350°F. Remove and unwrap 1 dough square. Using a 1-inch square cutter, cut out 24 cookies. Transfer to 2 parchment-lined baking pans, spacing cookies about 1 inch apart. Bake until light golden and firm around the edges, 12 to 15 minutes, rotating pans halfway through. Transfer cookies to a wire rack to cool completely. Repeat with remaining dough squares.
4. Dip cookies in glaze (recipes below) on the diagonal, then gently swipe bottom edge to remove excess. If specified below, sprinkle with toppings. Set cookies on wire rack placed atop a sheet of waxed paper. Allow glaze to completely harden overnight.
5. To package, remove dividers from 4 boxes and line the bottom of each box with parchment. Replace dividers. Arrange 24 cookies (6 of each glaze) in box, as shown at right.

GLAZES

Lemon Glaze
In a small bowl, combined **1½ cups confectioners' sugar, 3 tablespoons lemon juice**, and **1½ tablespoons corn syrup**. Dip cookies as directed, and sprinkle with **1 tablespoon lemon zest**.

Almond Glaze
In a small bowl, combine **1½ cups confectioners' sugar, 3 tablespoons milk, 1½ tablespoons corn syrup**, and **⅛ teaspoon almond extract**. Dip cookies as directed, and sprinkle with **1 tablespoon finely chopped toasted almonds**.

Blackberry Glaze
Press **1 cup frozen blackberries**, thawed, through a fine-mesh sieve to extract juices. In a small bowl, combine **3 tablespoons blackberry juice, 1½ cups confectioners' sugar**, and **1½ tablespoons corn syrup**. Dip cookies as directed.

White Chocolate–Pistachio Glaze
In a medium heatproof bowl set over a pot of simmering water, melt **8 ounces white chocolate** in **4 teaspoons vegetable shortening**. Remove bowl from heat and stir in **4 teaspoons pistachio paste** and **⅛ teaspoon fine sea salt**. Allow mixture to rest for 1 minute. Dip cookies as directed, and sprinkle with **1 tablespoon finely chopped pistachios.**

BRIGHT IDEA! Display in a clear-topped checkerboard box. The sturdy container can later hold other petite treasures like jewelry or sewing notions.

Shortbread Cookies

Bite-sized shortbread cookies dipped in fruity glazes, chopped nuts, and citrus zest pass for tiny works of art.

Cover small boxes with wrapping paper to get the look of handmade vintage containers.

Clockwise from top left:
Roly Polys,
Jam Thumbprints,
Red-and-Whites,
and Raspberry Bars.

◇◇◇

ONE TASTY RECIPE
YIELDS FOUR VERY DIFFERENT KINDS OF
CHRISTMAS COOKIES

◇◇◇◇◇◇◇◇◇◇◇◇◇◇◇◇◇◇◇◇◇◇◇◇◇◇◇◇

TEA COOKIE DOUGH

In a large bowl, using mixer set on high, beat **1 stick softened, unsalted butter** until fluffy. Add **½ cup confectioners' sugar, 1½ teaspoon vanilla extract, and ⅛ teaspoon salt.** Reduce mixer speed to low, and gradually add in **1¼ cups all-purpose flour.** Now you're ready to make the cookies that follow.

Roly Polys

Makes 24 cookies *Working time* 25 min. *Total time* 45 min.

Preheat oven to 325°F. Make **Tea Cookie Dough,** but stir in **⅔ cup finely chopped hazelnuts** once flour has been incorporated. Roll dough, by the tablespoon, into balls and place 1 inch apart on baking sheets. Bake until cookies are firm and just beginning to brown, about 20 minutes. Let cool for 2 minutes. Place **½ cup confectioners' sugar** in a shallow bowl, then gently toss warm cookies to coat. Transfer cookies to wire rack to cool completely. Toss cookies in confectioners' sugar one more time to coat thoroughly.

Jam Thumbprints

Makes 16 cookies *Working time* 20 min. *Total time* 1 hr. 40 min.

Preheat oven to 325°F. Make **Tea Cookie Dough.** Roll dough, 1½ tablespoons at a time, into balls. Pour **¼ cup granulated sugar** into a shallow bowl and toss balls to coat; place balls 1½ inches apart on a baking sheet. Press your thumb into center of each cookie to create a small well. Bake cookies until firm, 15 to 18 minutes. Remove from oven and further define well by pressing with your thumb. Transfer to a wire rack to cool. Fill well of each cookie with **½ teaspoon strawberry jelly,** then sprinkle jelly with **sugar.** Let cookies rest until jelly sets.

Red-and-Whites

Makes 10 cookies *Working time* 25 min. *Total time* 40 min.

Preheat oven to 350°F. Make **Tea Cookie Dough,** but substitute **½ cup granulated sugar** for **confectioners' sugar.** Once sugar and butter are blended, beat in **2 large egg yolks.** Divide dough into 10 equal portions and roll into balls. Place 3 inches apart on parchment-lined baking sheets and bake until edges are crisp, about 12 minutes. Cool completely on baking sheets. Meanwhile, make icing by mixing **1 cup confectioners' sugar** with **3 to 4 tablespoons cream.** Spread on cooled cookies to cover tops. Sprinkle half of each cookie with **red sugar.**

Raspberry Bars

Makes 9 bars *Working time* 25 min. *Total time* 1 hr. 15 min.

Preheat oven to 350°F. Make **Tea Cookie Dough,** but add an additional **¾ cup confectioners' sugar** to butter mixture. Once sugar and butter are blended, beat in **1 large egg.** Spread ¼ of batter (reserve the rest) in an 8-inch-square baking pan, then top with **¾ cup raspberry preserves.** Stir **¼ cup unsweetened coconut** into reserved batter, then drop batter in small dollops atop preserves. Bake until a toothpick inserted into center tests clean, 45 to 50 minutes. Cool in pan, then drizzle with **2 ounces melted white chocolate.** Once chocolate sets, cut into bars.

GINGERBREAD ANIMALS

Makes 4 boxes of 12 cookies **Working time** *40 min.* **Total time** *50 min., plus cooling and decorating*

COOKIES

3½ cups all-purpose flour, plus more for parchment and cutters
1 tablespoon ground ginger
1 teaspoon coriander
½ teaspoon ground cloves
½ teaspoon salt
1½ sticks unsalted butter
⅔ cup light brown sugar
½ cup dark corn syrup
¼ cup molasses

ROYAL ICING

4 cups confectioners' sugar
6 tablespoons warm water
3 tablespoons meringue powder
Brown, pink, and red gel food coloring

1. In a large bowl, combine flour, ginger, coriander, cloves, and salt. Set aside.
2. In a medium saucepan over medium heat, combine butter, brown sugar, corn syrup, and molasses; cook, stirring frequently, until blended. Pour into flour mixture, stirring with a wooden spoon until a smooth dough forms. Cover and refrigerate until cool enough to handle, about 1 hour.
3. Divide dough into 2 equal pieces and pat each into a square. Roll out each square between 2 sheets of lightly floured parchment to ¼-inch thickness. Transfer to a baking pan, wrap tightly with plastic wrap, and refrigerate 1 to 1½ hours.
4. Preheat oven to 350°F. Remove and unwrap 1 dough square. Using lightly floured cutters, cut out 6 each of pig, cow, rooster, and horse shapes. Transfer to 2 parchment-lined pans, spacing cookies about 1 inch apart. Bake until firm, 10 minutes, rotating pans halfway through. Transfer to a wire rack to cool completely. Repeat with remaining dough.

For Royal Icing
1. In a large bowl, using an electric mixer on high, beat confectioners' sugar, 6 tablespoons warm water, and 3 tablespoons meringue powder until thick and glossy, 10 to 12 minutes.
2. Divide icing among 4 bowls. To tint icing for pig cookies: Dip a toothpick ¾ inch deep into pink gel food coloring and stir into first bowl. For cow: Stir ¼ teaspoon brown gel food coloring into second bowl. For rooster: Stir ¼ teaspoon red gel food coloring into third bowl; dip a toothpick ¾ inch deep into brown gel food coloring and stir into icing. For horse: Leave fourth bowl white.
3. Decorate cookies with specified colors of Royal Icing. To package, nestle 12 cookies (3 of each animal shape) into each of 4 boxes.

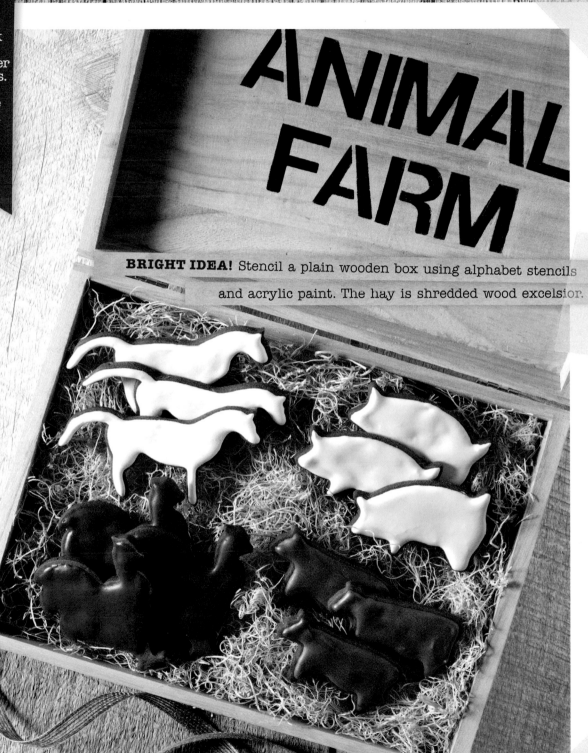

Traditional gingerbread takes a walk on the wild side, via critter cookie cutters. Corral the whole stable in a wooden box.

ANIMAL FARM

BRIGHT IDEA! Stencil a plain wooden box using alphabet stencils and acrylic paint. The hay is shredded wood excelsior.

DIY GINGERBREAD-HOUSE KIT

Makes 1 gift of 1 house kit **Working time** *30 min.*
Total time *1 hr. 40 min., plus chilling*

6¾	cups all-purpose flour
2	tablespoons ground ginger
1	teaspoon ground allspice
1	teaspoon ground cloves
½	teaspoon salt
1½	cups light corn syrup
1½	cups dark brown sugar
1½	cups vegetable shortening
2½	cups confectioners' sugar
4	teaspoons meringue powder

1. In a large bowl, combine the first
5 ingredients. In a medium pot over medium
heat, combine corn syrup, brown sugar,
and vegetable shortening. Stir until sugar
dissolves and shortening melts. Pour the
sugar-shortening mixture into the dry-
ingredients mixture and, using a wooden
spoon, stir until dough forms. Let rest until
cool enough to handle, about 20 minutes.
2. Divide dough into 4 equal pieces. Place
each piece of dough between 2 sheets of
parchment and roll until ¼ inch thick. Transfer
to a baking sheet, cover tightly with plastic
wrap, and refrigerate for about 3 hours.
3. Preheat oven to 350°F. Meanwhile, line
3 baking sheets with parchment and set
aside. Remove dough from refrigerator and
unwrap. Using the templates (at countryliving.
com/gingerbread) and a pizza cutter, cut
out 2 side, 2 front/back, and 2 roof pieces
from the dough. Transfer pieces to prepared
baking sheets and refrigerate for 15 minutes.
Remove from refrigerator and bake until firm,
30 minutes, rotating sheets halfway through.
Transfer to a wire rack to cool completely.
4. For icing mix: In a medium bowl, stir
confectioners' sugar and meringue powder
to combine.

BRIGHT IDEA!

TO PACKAGE, wrap
gingerbread pieces
individually in
parchment, and
transfer icing mix to
snack-size resealable
plastic bags; then
slide each inside a
5-inch-wide by
7½-inch-high bag
(ours are made of
notebook paper).
PLACE dragées and
other candies inside
2¾-inch-wide by
4-inch-high grid-
paper-patterned
bags. SECURE all
bags with ruler-
print washi tape.
FOR FREE house-
assembly instruction
card, go to
countryliving.com
/gingerbreadlabels.
PRINT label, cut out,
and adhere with
spray adhesive to
the center of the
front of a 9½-inch-
wide by 5-inch-high
by 5-inch-deep gable
box. LINE BOX with
shredded kraft
paper. THEN place
instruction card and
bagged gingerbread
pieces, icing mix,
and candies inside.

This adorable kit gives the recipient a head start on creating a wonderful holiday tradition.

{143}

HOW TO ASSEMBLE YOUR · GINGERBREAD HOUSE ·

PREPARE THE ICING Add three tablespoons water and beat until thick and lightly glossy.

BUILD THE HOUSE Use the icing as "mortar" to join the gingerbread pieces that form the house's sides, front, and back, supporting the pieces with canned goods while you work. Let the icing set for two hours, then attach gingerbread pieces that form the roof. Let the icing set. (Note: Prevent the icing from drying out when not in use, cover with plastic wrap, pressing film directly onto icing.)

DECORATE THE HOUSE Use remaining icing to adhere candy and cookies to the house. You can also use icing to pipe designs onto the house. Fill the icing with a teaspoon or two of water. Transfer to a resealable plastic bag, snip off one bottom corner, and press gently to release icing.

BRIGHT IDEA! To package, place 4 cheesecakes in a 6⅝-inch-diameter, 1¹³⁄₁₆-inch-high tin; place crumpled parchment between cheesecakes. Tie top of tin with tartan ribbon (as shown) before closing.

A sweet pecan topping and buttery shortbread crust make the recipient of these morsels very merry indeed.

MINI CHEESECAKES WITH SUGARED PECANS

Makes 4 gifts of 4 cheesecakes each (16 cheesecakes total) *Working time* 20 min. *Total time* 1 hr., plus chilling

- 1 cup finely crushed shortbread cookies, such as Lorna Doone
- ⅓ cup finely chopped pecans, plus ½ cup coarsely chopped pecans
- 2 tablespoons light brown sugar
- ⅛ teaspoon fine salt, plus ½ teaspoon
- 1 tablespoon butter, melted
- 2 packages (8 ounces each) cream cheese, at room temperature
- 1 cup granulated sugar
- 2 tablespoons flour
- 2 large eggs
- 1½ teaspoons vanilla extract

1. Preheat oven to 300°F. Meanwhile, line 16 standard muffin-tin cups with paper liners and set aside. In a medium bowl, stir together cookie crumbs, finely chopped pecans, brown sugar, and ⅛ teaspoon salt. Stir in melted butter until mixture resembles wet sand. Evenly divide among prepared muffin cups and press down to form a solid bottom layer. Bake until set, 5 to 8 minutes. Transfer pans to wire racks to cool completely.

2. Meanwhile, in a large bowl, using an electric mixer on medium speed, beat together cream cheese and ¾ cup granulated sugar until blended. Beat in flour and remaining salt. Beat in eggs, one at a time, and vanilla. Divide filling equally among the muffin cups. Bake until set, 16 to 18 minutes. Transfer pans to wire racks to cool completely, then refrigerate cheesecakes for at least 3 hours or up to overnight.

3. Meanwhile, oil a piece of parchment and set aside. In a small skillet over medium heat, stir coarsely chopped pecans and remaining sugar together until sugar melts and is bubbling, and nuts are coated. Transfer to prepared parchment, separate any nuts that are stuck together, and let cool. Right before gifting, remove cheesecakes from refrigerator and top each with about 1½ teaspoons candied pecans, to garnish.

Decidedly mature flavors, including coffee and lavender, lend these melt-in-your-mouth delicacies a sophisticated profile.

peppermint

chocolate

coffee

lavender

BRIGHT IDEA! Show marshmallows to their best advantage in a simple glassine bag tied with a length of dapper ribbon.

GOURMET MARSHMALLOWS

Makes 12 marshmallows per flavor (4 batches yield 16 bags of 3 marshmallows, 4 bags of each variation) **Working time** 40 min. **Total time** 55 min., plus resting

¼ cup confectioners' sugar
¼ cup cornstarch
    Vegetable oil, for pan
2 envelopes (¼ ounce each) unflavored gelatin
1½ cups granulated sugar
⅔ cup light corn syrup

1. In a small bowl, sift together confectioners' sugar and cornstarch; set aside. Brush the bottom and sides of an 8-inch-square baking pan with vegetable oil. Cut an 8- by 12-inch sheet of parchment and fit into pan so that it covers bottom and 2 sides. Brush parchment with oil, and coat parchment and pan with half of the confectioners' sugar mixture. Set aside.
2. Fill a large bowl with ½ cup cool water and sprinkle with gelatin; set aside. In a medium pot fitted with a candy thermometer, combine granulated sugar, corn syrup, and ½ cup water; bring to a boil over high heat. Reduce heat to medium and cook until mixture reaches 240°F, 7 to 10 minutes. Remove from heat and set aside.
3. Using an electric mixer, beat reserved gelatin mixture on low for about 30 seconds, then pour in reserved sugar–corn syrup mixture in a slow, steady stream down side of bowl. Increase mixer speed to high and beat until very thick, ribbony, and doubled in volume, 12 to 15 minutes.
4. Pour batter into prepared pan. Using dampened fingers, smooth top. Sprinkle remaining confectioners' sugar mixture over top. Let rest, uncovered, in a cool, dry place, about 4 hours or up to overnight.

5. Invert marshmallow onto a dry surface and discard parchment. Using a clean, dry pastry brush, dust excess confectioners' sugar from the top of the marshmallow onto work surface. Dust a knife in confectioners' sugar from the work surface, then cut the marshmallow into twelve 1¾-inch squares (you'll have a bit extra). Dip the cut edges in the excess confectioners' sugar mixture on the work surface. To package, divide 1 batch among 4 bags, placing 3 marshmallows in each bag. Repeat with batches of the other variations.

VARIATIONS
Peppermint Marshmallows
After completing Step 2, add **1 teaspoon mint extract** and beat for 30 seconds.

Chocolate Marshmallows
Before beginning steps: In a small bowl, mix together **6 tablespoons cocoa** and **3 tablespoons hot water** until a smooth paste forms; set aside. In Step 1, sift **¼ cup cocoa** with confectioners' sugar and cornstarch. In Step 3, beat reserved cocoa paste into reserved gelatin mixture before adding sugar mixture.

Lavender Marshmallows
Before beginning steps: In a small saucepan over high heat, bring **1 cup water** and **2 tablespoons lavender** to a boil. Set aside and let steep for 20 minutes. Strain and reserve liquid; discard lavender. In Step 2, substitute reserved lavender water in both instances where water is called for.

Coffee Marshmallows
Before beginning steps: In a small bowl, dissolve **6 tablespoons instant espresso** in **1 cup boiling water**. Set aside to cool to room temperature. In Step 2, substitute reserved espresso in both instances where water is called for.

A cinch to make using a sectioned mold and chocolate melts, these candy bars only look professional—especially when wrapped in gorgeous papers and artisanal-chic labels.

TART-CHERRY & DARK-CHOCOLATE BARS

Makes 4 bars *Working time* 15 min.
Total time 25 min.

8   ounces dark-chocolate candy melts, preferably Guittard Melt 'n Mold
¼   cup chopped dried tart cherries

1. In a double boiler set over simmering water, heat chocolate, stirring frequently, until melted, about 5 minutes.

2. Fill four 5⅜- by 2⅛- by ⅛-inch candy bar molds halfway with chocolate. Divide cherries among molds; cover with remaining chocolate. Using a small offset spatula, smooth tops. Lightly tap molds on work surface to remove any air bubbles.

3. Refrigerate until set, 5 to 10 minutes. Remove and release chocolate bars. Store in an airtight container in a cool, dry place until ready to wrap, up to 4 weeks.

BRIGHT IDEA! Download the labels shown here formatted to fit an 8½-inch-wide by 11-inch-long sheet of sticker paper at countryliving.com/chocolatelabels. Just print onto kraft paper stickers and cut.

Presentation is everything:
Deliver loaves in darling—and
cheap!—little bread pans. When
gifted in a glass dish, the butter
looks twice as nice.

MINI COUNTRY LOAVES

Makes 4 loaves **Working time** *30 min.*
Total time *3 hr. 30 min.*

1   package dry active yeast
2   tablespoons sugar
3   cups all-purpose flour, plus more
     for kneading
⅔   cup warm (110°F) milk
½   cup old-fashioned oats, plus 2
     tablespoons for sprinkling
1½ teaspoons fine sea salt
2   large egg yolks
2   tablespoons olive oil
¼   cup warm water, or more
     (up to ½ cup), as needed
1   egg white, lightly beaten

1. In a medium bowl, combine yeast, sugar, 1 cup flour, and milk. Cover bowl with a towel; let yeast mixture rise until doubled in volume, about 1 hour.

2. Using a food processor, grind oats into a fine flour. Add sea salt and remaining 2 cups flour; pulse to combine. With motor running, add yeast mixture, egg yolks, and olive oil. Drizzle in water until dough forms.

3. Remove dough and knead on a lightly floured surface until supple, about 4 minutes. Place in a large, well-oiled bowl, turning dough to coat with oil. Cover bowl with a towel; let dough rise until doubled in volume, about 1 hour.

4. Heat oven to 400°F. Punch down dough and knead for 1 minute. Divide into 4 equal portions; shape into loaves to fit into 5 ¾- by 3¼- by 2-inch pans. Cover pans with a towel for 20 minutes.

5. Place loaves on baking sheet, lightly brush tops with egg white, and sprinkle with remaining oats. Bake until golden, 25 minutes. Cool completely.

SWEETEN THE DEAL BY MAKING **FRESH BUTTER!**

Makes 12 oz. **Working time** *20 min.* **Total time** *20 min.*

In a blender on medium speed, mix **4 cups heavy cream** and **1½ teaspoons coarse salt (preferably fleur de sel)** until grainy milk curds begin to form, 8 to 10 minutes. Meanwhile, set aside **2 cups ice water.** Pour milk curds through a strainer (discard liquid) and transfer to a chilled bowl. Pour **½ cup ice water** over curds and, using a rubber spatula, press out any residual liquid, or whey. Drain water when it gets cloudy, then add more water **(½ cup at a time)**, press out more liquid, and drain. Repeat 1 or 2 times more until water stays clear. Now you have butter. Divide it into four 3-ounce dome glass dishes or roll into logs and wrap in parchment paper. Refrigerate.

GOLDEN HONEY GRANOLA

Makes 15 cups **Working time** *15 min.*
Total time *55 min.*

1	container (18-ounce) old-fashioned oats (6 cups)
8	ounces sliced almonds
1	cup dried cranberries
1	cup chopped dried apricots
1	cup light brown sugar
1	teaspoon ground cinnamon
½	teaspoon salt
1½	sticks unsalted butter
½	cup honey

1. Preheat oven to 350°F. In a large bowl, toss together all ingredients except butter and honey.

2. In a small saucepan over medium heat, melt butter. Stir in honey. Pour over oat mixture and toss to distribute. Spread granola onto a parchment-lined baking sheet and bake, stirring occasionally, until oats are toasted and sugar begins to caramelize, 35 to 40 minutes. Cool completely on sheet. Transfer to an airtight container.

BRIGHT IDEA! Package granola in pretty jars and add a cute scoop for good measure!

Happy Holidays

BASIC QUICK BREAD DOUGH

Working time 10 min. *Total time* 10 min.

3   cups all-purpose flour
1   tablespoon baking powder
2   teaspoons salt
4   large eggs
1   cup whole milk
6   tablespoons unsalted
    butter, melted

In a large bowl, combine flour, baking powder, and salt. In a medium bowl, lightly beat together eggs and milk. Pour milk mixture and melted butter into dry ingredients and stir until just combined.

VARIATIONS

Banana, Brown Sugar, and White Chocolate Mini-Bundt Cakes

Makes 24 mini-Bundt cakes
Working time 25 min. *Total time* 1 hr.

3   very ripe bananas, mashed
1   cup packed light-brown sugar
6   ounces chopped white chocolate
1   teaspoon vanilla extract
½   teaspoon ground nutmeg
    Basic Quick Bread Dough
    (recipe above)

1. Preheat oven to 350°F. In a large bowl, beat bananas, sugar, chocolate, vanilla, and nutmeg. Stir mixture into Basic Quick Bread Dough until combined. Coat a 12-cup mini-Bundt pan with cooking spray. Spoon 3 tablespoons batter into each cup.

2. Bake until a skewer tests clean when inserted into the center, 18 to 20 minutes. Remove cakes from pan and let cool on a wire rack. Repeat to make second batch.

Dried Plum and Apple Loaf with Crumble Topping

Makes 1 loaf (about 12 servings) *Working time* 20 min. *Total time* 1 hr. 20 min.

    Basic Quick Bread Dough
    (recipe left)
¾   cup sugar
1   tablespoon sugar, for crumble
    topping
1   large Granny Smith apple, peeled,
    cored, and finely chopped
¾   cup pitted chopped dried plums
1   teaspoon ground cinnamon
¾   cup granola
2   tablespoons unsalted butter,
    softened
2   tablespoons all-purpose flour

1. Preheat oven to 350°F. Combine Basic Quick Bread Dough and ¾ cup sugar, apple, plums, and cinnamon. Transfer to a nonstick 9- by 5-inch loaf pan.

2. For crumble topping: In a small bowl, combine granola, butter, flour, and remaining 1 tablespoon sugar. Sprinkle over dough.

3. Bake until a skewer tests clean when inserted into the center, about 1 hour. Remove loaf from pan and let cool on a wire rack.

A no-fuss, no-knead dough serves as the foundation for these sweet and savory loaves—all of which take about an hour to make.

Dried Plum and Apple Loaf with Crumble Topping

Bacon-Cheddar Mini Loaf
{recipe on p.156}

Banana, Brown Sugar, and White Chocolate Mini-Bundt Cakes

Glazed Orange-Poppy Mini Loaf
{recipe on p.156}

Mixed-Olive Loaf
{recipe on p.156}

Bacon-Cheddar Mini Loaves

Makes *4 mini loaves (about 12 servings)*
Working time *25 mins.* *Total time* *1 hr.*

8	slices bacon, cooked and chopped (2 teaspoons bacon fat reserved)
1	cup finely chopped onion
2	cups grated sharp Cheddar
	Basic Quick Bread Dough (recipe on p. 154)

1. Preheat oven to 350 °F. In a large nonstick skillet over medium-low heat, heat bacon fat. Add onion and cook until soft and translucent, about 8 minutes; let cool.

2. Add onion, bacon, and 1½ cups Cheddar to Basic Quick Bread Dough and stir until combined. Transfer to 4 nonstick mini-loaf pans (5¾ by 3 inches). Sprinkle top of each loaf with ½ cup Cheddar.

3. Bake until a skewer tests clean when inserted into the center, 30 to 35 minutes. Remove loaves from pans and let cool on a wire rack.

Glazed Orange-Poppy Mini Loaves

Makes *4 mini loaves (about 12 servings)*

	Basic Quick Bread Dough (recipe on p. 154)
2	cups granulated sugar
3	tablespoons poppy seeds
	Zest of 2 oranges
2	tablespoons fresh orange juice
1	cup confectioners' sugar

1. Preheat oven to 350°F. Combine Basic Quick Bread Dough and sugar, poppy seeds, and orange zest. Transfer to 4 nonstick mini-loaf pans (5¾ by 3 inches).

2. Bake until a skewer tests clean when inserted into the center, 30 to 35 minutes. Remove loaves from pans and let cool on a wire rack. In a small bowl, mix juice and confectioners' sugar until smooth. Spoon evenly over tops of loaves.

Mixed Olive Loaf

Makes *1 loaf (about 12 servings)*
Working time *15 min.* *Total time* *1 hr.*

	Basic Quick Bread Dough (recipe on p. 154)
½	cup pitted chopped Kalamata olives, plus 1 tablespoon
½	cup Picholine olives, plus 1 tablespoon
1½	teaspoons fresh thyme
1	teaspoon ground cumin

1. Preheat oven to 350°F. Combine Basic Quick Bread Dough and ½ cup each Kalamata and Picholine olives, thyme, and cumin. Transfer to a nonstick 9- by 5-inch loaf pan. Sprinkle remaining 2 tablespoons olives over top.

2. Bake until a skewer tests clean when inserted into the center, 45 minutes. Remove loaf from pan and let cool on a wire rack.

Olive loaf dough: For the tenderest loaves, use a light hand when mixing the ingredients and bake the bread right away.

PRETZELS WITH BROWN-SUGAR ROSEMARY DIJON

Makes 4 gifts of 6 pretzels each (24 pretzels total) **Working time** 1 hr. 10 min. **Total time** 2 hr. 40 min.

3	tablespoons honey
1½	packages (about 3¼ teaspoons) active dry yeast
5¼	cups all-purpose flour, plus at least another ½ cup for kneading
¾	cups whole-wheat flour
1½	teaspoons fine salt, plus a pinch for egg whites
6	tablespoons olive oil, plus more for coating bowl
6	tablespoons baking soda
2	large egg whites
3½	tablespoons coarse sea salt

1. In a medium bowl, combine 1 tablespoon honey, yeast, and 2¼ cups warm water (100°F), and stir until yeast dissolves; let sit until foamy, about 5 minutes.
2. Meanwhile, in a large bowl, combine flours and fine salt. Using a wooden spoon, stir in the oil, yeast mixture, and remaining honey until a shaggy dough forms. Sprinkle ½ cup flour on your work surface, then transfer dough to surface and knead, adding up to ½ cup more flour as needed, until dough becomes supple and elastic.
3. Coat a large, clean bowl with olive oil. Place the dough in the bowl, and cover with a towel. Let rise in a warm place until dough doubles in volume, about 1 hour.
4. Line 2 baking pans with parchment and set aside. Punch dough down and knead for 5 minutes. Divide dough into twenty-four 1½-ounce pieces (each slightly larger than a golf ball) and keep covered. Working with one piece at a time, roll dough into a 14-inch-long rope. Bring both ends together and twist twice near the top. Fold ends down so they sit atop the bottom loop of dough; press ends into loop to form a pretzel. Transfer to a prepared pan and repeat with remaining dough. Let pretzels rest for 15 minutes.
5. Preheat oven to 400°F. Meanwhile, in a medium pot, bring 6 cups water and baking soda to a rapid simmer. Working in batches, poach pretzels for about 15 seconds on each side. Return to prepared pans. Lightly beat egg whites with a pinch of fine salt. Then lightly brush pretzels with the egg-white mixture and sprinkle with coarse salt. Bake until pretzels are deep brown and cooked through, about 15 minutes. Transfer to a wire rack to cool completely.

BRIGHT IDEA!

Place each pretzel into a 5-inch-wide by 7½-inch-high kraft dot bag and seal with a red circle sticker. DIVIDE mustard among four 4-ounce glass jars. PLACE a kraft sticker label on each jar and use a black Sharpie to label as shown. PLACE 6 pretzels and 1 jar of mustard inside a wooden planter box. WITH the same Sharpie, write a message on a wooden tag and tie it to the box.

To kick up store-bought mustard, just stir 4 tablespoons light-brown sugar and 2 tablespoons finely chopped rosemary into 2 2/3 cups Dijon mustard.

SAVORY CRACKERS

Makes 60 crackers per batch
*(3 batches yield 4 boxes of 45
crackers, 15 of each variation)*
Working time 30 min.
Total time 40 min., plus chilling

1½ cups all-purpose flour
2   tablespoons nonfat dry milk
1   teaspoon fine salt
1   stick unsalted butter, cold and
     cut into small pieces
1½ cups (about 6 ounces)
     coarsely grated cheese

1. In the bowl of a food processor,
pulse flour, dry milk, and salt. Add
butter and pulse until mixture
resembles wet sand. Add cheese
and pulse until combined. Drizzle
in 4 to 6 tablespoons ice water,
pulsing just until dough begins to
come together.
2. Roll dough into an 8-inch-long
log. Divide dough into 2 equal-size
logs, wrap both tightly in plastic
wrap, and refrigerate for at least
3 hours.
3. Preheat oven to 325°F. Meanwhile, remove and unwrap 1 log.
Using a wire cheese cutter, slice
log into thirty ⊠-inch-thick rounds.
Transfer to 2 parchment-lined
baking pans (preferably insulated),
spacing rounds about 1 inch apart.
4. Bake until golden brown, 10 to
12 minutes, rotating pans halfway
through. Transfer crackers to a wire
rack to cool completely.
5. Repeat Steps 3 and 4 with
remaining log. To package, line the

compartments of 4 boxes with
parchment. Divide 1 batch among
the boxes, placing 15 crackers in one
compartment of each box. Repeat
with batches of other variations.

VARIATIONS

Walnut-Parmesan Crackers

In Step 1, select **Parmesan** for
cheese. After Step 2, place **½ cup
finely chopped walnuts** (about
2½ ounces) in a shallow bowl.
In Step 3, lightly press 1 side of
each round into walnuts before
transferring, nut side up, to
baking pans.

Gouda Crackers with Poppy and Sesame Seeds

In Step 1, select **smoked Gouda** for
cheese. After Step 2, in a shallow
bowl, combine **2 tablespoons
poppy seeds, 1 tablespoon
sesame seeds, 1 tablespoon
kosher salt,** and **½ tablespoon
each garlic powder and onion
powder**. In Step 3, lightly press
1 side of each round into seed-spice
mixture before transferring, seed
side up, to baking pans.

Chili-Cheddar Cornmeal Crackers

In Step 1, add **¼ cup white
cornmeal** and **2 teaspoons chili
powder** to dry ingredients and
select **Cheddar** for cheese.

SPICY COCKTAIL PECANS

Makes 4 bags *Working time* 5 min.
Total time 40 min.

1   stick unsalted butter, melted
4   teaspoons Tabasco sauce
2   teaspoons Worcestershire
     sauce
2   teaspoons sea salt
1   teaspoon garlic powder
6   cups (about 1½ pounds) pecan
     halves

1. Preheat oven to 325°F with racks
set in the top and middle positions.
Meanwhile, in a small bowl, stir
together all ingredients except
pecans.

2. Place pecans in a large bowl.
Pour butter mixture over pecans,
tossing to combine. Spread pecans
evenly on 2 baking pans and bake
until toasted and fragrant, 12 to
15 minutes, rotating pans halfway
through. Transfer to a paper-
towel–lined baking pan and let
cool completely, 20 minutes. To
package, place 1½ cups pecans in
each of 4 lined kraft paper bags.

BRIGHT IDEA!

Log onto countryliving
.com/pecanlabels for the
label graphics, designed
to fit an 8½-inch-wide
by 11-inch-long sheet
of cardstock. Just print
and cut with pinking
shears!

Spicy
Cocktail
Pecans

Spicy
Cocktail
Pecans

All you need to bake this delicious snack? Twenty minutes and six common ingredients (Tabasco, Worcestershire, garlic powder, salt, butter, and pecans). Stash the nuts in a brown paper bag brightened by cheery fabric, twine, and a pinking-sheared label—plus a jaunty clothespin.

This trio of slice-and-bake crisps gets its cheesy richness from Parmesan, Gouda, and Cheddar. A divided wood box delivers ready-to-serve ease.

Walnut and Parmesan

Gouda with Poppy and Sesame Seeds

Chili-Cheddar Cornmeal

BRIGHT IDEA! Shred old newspapers or book pages for inexpensive, earth-friendly packing materials. Visit countryliving.com/saltlabels for the typewriter labels shown, formatted to fit an 8½-inch-wide by 11-inch-long sheet of sticker paper.

Porcini Salt

Smoked Paprika & Ancho Salt

Celery Salt

Lime-Ginger Salt

Herbes de Provence Salt

Curry Salt

The most basic of seasonings turns truly gift-worthy when you incorporate wild mushrooms, ancho chilies, or garam masala—then arrange it all in cute-as-can-be jars sporting typewriter-style labels. A sleek metal tin completes the set.

FLAVORED SALTS

Makes 4 tins of 6 jars (4 of each flavor)

For each of the methods below, divide the finished salt among 4 two-ounce jars, and tighten lids to seal. To package, fill 4 tins with shredded paper; in each tin, nestle 6 jars of different flavored salts.

Porcini Salt: Using a spice grinder, and working in batches if necessary, pulse **dried porcini mushrooms** until finely ground. In a medium bowl, combine ground porcini and sea salt.

Smoked Paprika and Ancho Salt: Remove stems and seeds of **dried ancho chiles**. Using a mortar and pestle, break up chiles. Using a spice grinder, and working in batches if necessary, pulse until coarsely ground. In a medium bowl, combine ground chiles, **smoked paprika**, and fine sea salt.

Celery Salt: Preheat oven to 250°F. Place leaves from **4 heads of celery** on 2 parchment-lined baking pans and bake until dry, about 10 minutes. Let cool completely. Using a spice grinder, and working in batches if necessary, pulse until coarsely ground. In a medium bowl, combine ground celery leaves and fine sea salt.

Lime-Ginger Salt: Spread **lime zest** on waxed paper; let dry overnight. In a medium bowl, combine lime zest, **ground ginger**, and fine sea salt.

Herbes de Provence Salt: Using a spice grinder, and working in batches if necessary, pulse **herbes de Provence** and **lavender** until coarsely ground. In a medium bowl, combine ground herbes de Provence and lavender and fine sea salt.

Curry Salt: Using a mortar and pestle, crush **bay leaves** until coarsely ground. In a medium bowl, combine ground bay leaves with **garam masala**, **curry powder**, **ground cumin**, and fine sea salt.

ROSEMARY HONEY

Makes 4 jars **Working time** 25 min.
Total time 1 hr. 5 min.

8   cups mild honey
10 springs rosemary, rinsed and dried

1. In a medium saucepan over low heat, cook honey and 6 sprigs rosemary just until honey begins to bubble around the edges. Remove from heat and let steep for 20 minutes.
2. Using tongs, remove and discard rosemary sprigs and any stray leaves. To decant, divide honey among 4 clean 16-ounce jars. Let cool completely, about 40 minutes. Insert 1 fresh sprig rosemary into each jar, and tighten lids to seal.

> Transform store-bought honey with an aromatic sprig and sweet bee art.

BRIGHT IDEA! Print 10 bee images (at countryliving.com/honeylabels) per 8½-inch-wide by 11-inch-long sheet of clear, oval stickers.

If you really want to boost someone's holiday spirits, steep vodka with tangy hibiscus, refreshing cucumber and lime, or zesty horseradish. Decant your handiwork in beautiful bottles that cost about a buck apiece.

INFUSED VODKAS
Makes 12 bottles (4 of each flavor)

For each of the methods below, use a 2-gallon pitcher to combine **four 750-milliliter bottles of vodka** and specified flavorings; steep as directed. To decant, use a funnel to divide the finished vodka among four clean 750-milliliter bottles, then seal with corks.

Hibiscus-Infused Vodka: Steep **8 pure hibiscus tea bags**, tags removed, in vodka for four hours; strain, then decant.

Cucumber-Lime-Infused Vodka: Peel **1 seedless English cucumber**. Refrigerate peel, and slice cucumber into ¼-inch-thick rounds. Cut the peel of **1 lime** into strips. Add cucumber rounds and lime peel to vodka; steep for 24 hours. Strain, then decant. Add **3 or 4 pieces of cucumber peel** to each bottle before corking.

Horseradish-Infused Vodka: Slice **8 ounces fresh horseradish root** into ¼-inch-thick rounds. Add horseradish rounds and **2 teaspoons whole black peppercorns** to vodka. Steep for 24 hours. Strain, then decant. Slice **1 ounce fresh horseradish root** into matchsticks. Add **5 or 6 matchsticks** and **3 or 4 peppercorns** to each bottle before corking

ESPRESSO-FLAVORED SUGAR CUBES
Makes 1 gift of 180 sugar cubes **Working time** 15 min. **Total time** 55 min., plus drying

Preheat oven to 250°F. Meanwhile, in a large bowl, combine **espresso powder**, **meringue powder**, and **hot water**. Whisk until no lumps remain; let cool. Add **sugar** and whisk until the mixture resembles damp sand. Spoon half of the sugar mixture into a 90-compartment silicone mini-ice-cube tray. Using a rubber spatula, spread the mixture, pressing it tightly into the tray's compartments. Scrape away any excess sugar mixture and return to bowl. Repeat with remaining sugar mixture and a second tray. Place trays on a baking sheet and bake for 40 minutes. Allow cubes to rest until hardened, about 8 hours, before carefully releasing from trays.

BRIGHT IDEA!

USE a black Sharpie and letter stencils to label 5-inch-wide by 7-inch-high jute bags, using the photo as a guide. DRAW a line above and below the label, as shown. WITH a red Sharpie, freehand a star at the top. TRANSFER the cubes to a 4¾-inch-wide by 6¾-inch-high cellophane bag, secure with a twist tie, and place inside the stenciled bag. Pull string to close.

Whimsically patterned paper is perfectly complemented by a red satin ribbon.

Wrap It Up! Good Things Come in Pretty Packages

It may be the thought that counts, but appealing paper and ribbon certainly up the ante. When shopping for distinctive purchased giftwrap, keep an eye out for unusual prints and colors. Or make your own! With just a little added flair, everyday materials can be standouts under the tree.

BROWN PAPER PACKAGES...

"My Favorite Things" had it right. Brown paper packages can hold their own with the fanciest gift-wrap—especially when they take on holiday shapes, or are gussied up with stamps, ribbons, and herbal bouquets.

This kraft paper wrapping was purchased already stamped.

Kraft paper and thread are all it takes to make this packaging designed with soft goods in mind. SIMPLY layer two pieces of kraft paper together, draw your chosen shape on the top piece, and cut through both layers of paper. SANDWICH a gift between the two shapes and stitch along the edges using contrasting thread.

{1}

{2}

{4}

{3}

GIFT TOPPERS

These colorful creations add a wow factor to humble brown wrapping paper.

{1}

HONEYCOMB ORNAMENTS

CUT 1½-inch and 2½-inch half circles from honeycomb paper. HOT-GLUE one side of folded half circle to package; unfold and glue other side of sphere to box. USE a silver paint pen to draw ornament hangers.

{2}

PAPER STRAW CHRISTMAS TREE

USE a pencil to draw a triangle on the top of the package. CUT paper straws in graduated lengths to fit horizontally within triangle. ADHERE with hot glue. CUT two 1-inch pieces of straw and glue vertically at base to form a trunk. WEAVE a piece of string down the length of tree, adhering with dots of hot glue. GLUE small buttons along length of string.

{3}

CANDY CANE SLEDS

WRAP a wood scrap measuring approximately 4-inch-wide by 1½-inch-high. GLUE a candy cane to either side and stack 1 to 2 small packages on top. TIE boxes and block with decorative ribbon to secure.

{4}

YARN POM-POM

TWIRL yarn around 4 fingers 50 times. CUT excess yarn and slide loop off fingers, making sure that it doesn't unravel. CINCH at middle with yarn. USE scissors to cut loops and fluff with fingers. WRAP package with coordinating yarn, using ends to tie on pom-pom.

Freebie road maps and atlas pages
serve as great graphic gift wrap.
Instead of tying a bow on top, thread
thin cord through a vintage button and
knot tightly to secure.

READ ALL ABOUT IT

Repurpose old newsprint, maps, and other printed matter as gift wrap and you'll be eco-friendly as well as stylish. Pair with simple twine, or splash out with fancy metallic ribbon. The beauty of these versatile wrappings is that everything works.

Wrap your gifts in nostalgic charm using vintage newsprint tied with lustrous silver rickrack, glittering snowflakes, and cherished family photos.

Butcher paper becomes the perfect backdrop for stag silhouettes. Print and cut out the template at countryliving.com/deershapes, then trace onto newsprint or construction paper and cut out. Tape in place and finish with twine.

Homemade paper cut into flower petals makes a subtle floral statement.

PLANT A GORGEOUS IDEA

Save the Santa paper for the kids and wrap grown-up gifts in beautiful botanicals, like these purchased papers. Check out specialty stores or websites such as katespaperie.com for unusual wares.

Not the usual suspects, these sophisticated botanical papers feature pines and pinecones, winter spores, and ferns.

Botanicals become even lovelier in shades of blue, chartreuse, silver, and gold, while faux bois takes a photo-realistic turn in this luxe burl-wood wrap.

SOFT TOUCH

Not all Christmas presents have to be decked out in bold red and green. Pastel lavenders and blues, as well as creams and golds, can get in the spirit on their own—or pair with candy cane stripes.

Try a softer, gentler palette for your wrappings this year, like this lovely grouping of creams, faded reds, lilacs, and golds.

Less conventional color combinations can be festive too. See how perfectly these lavender and periwinkle ribbons complement classic red and white vintage candy boxes.

Washburn's
ALL HARD CANDIES
MISTLETOE MIXTURE

THINK PINK—AND GREEN!

The traditional preppy colors can play it both ways—as heavenly pastels, or eye-popping brights. Either choice winks a bit at the expected red and green, and delivers a heaping helping of Christmas cheer.

Brighten up someone's holiday with bold hot pink and lime-green packages.

GOLDEN DAYS

Gold is a classic holiday hue. Using it in abundance makes a sumptuous statement perfectly in keeping with this festive, often luxurious, time of year.

To embellish but not overpower a diminutive package with an ample bow, choose diaphanous ribbon in a shade that allows the pattern of the wrapping paper to show through—such as this lovely example.

Presents wrapped in gleaming gold carry sentiments as precious as the gifts themselves. Glowing gilt leaves, twisted into a delicate wreath, add exquisite shimmer to gifts or on their own.

Use the Basic Sugar-Cookie Dough recipe on p.130 to make these candy-cane shaped treats.

PART THREE

Recipes for Celebrations

Sparkling Winter Sangria is a superb way to toast the holidays. For the recipe, see p. 190.

Holiday Cheer: Four Festive Party Ideas

There's something about Christmas that says "party time." Maybe it's old friends and beloved relatives coming to town for the holidays. Maybe it's the chilly weather that calls for warm celebrations. Or maybe it's just the infectious spirit of joy that spreads throughout the season. Whatever the reason, there's no better time of year for a get-together, whether simple or sumptuous. Be inspired by the menus and decorating ideas for the four festive holiday affairs that follow.

Podda Classico
This nutty cheese tastes great served alongside salty potato chips and champagne.

Roquefort
A funky blue cheese with a pungent flavor.

Sopressata
This Italian meat goes well with many cheeses, and lasts a long time in the fridge.

Fromager d'Affinois
A popular, soft, brie-like selection.

Marcona Almonds
A variety of almonds that is wonderfully salty and rich.

Carr's Table Water Crackers
A simple choice that never competes with other flavors.

Take a relaxed approach to holiday entertaining with an open-house party. Invite friends to drop by to enjoy appetizers and other finger food, as well as punch or a cocktail. Stock up on inexpensive glassware from Ikea, and cue the holiday playlist!

Picholine Olives
These mild olives are delicious on their own or in martinis.

Plum Chutney
Homemade condiments elevate your offerings.

Cheese Straws
A welcome Southern addition to the buffet table.

You can't go wrong with a cheese-and-charcuterie board. Simply unwrap these perfectly paired picks and—voila!—instant crowd-pleaser.

ROLL WITH THE PUNCHES

Mix up one hot punch and one cold libation and you can skip the fuss of preparing individual drinks.

"ALE"MENTS

Peel, core, and quarter **8 apples**. Tie up **5 cardamom pods**, **2 cinnamon sticks**, and **1 star anise** in a piece of cheesecloth. Place apples and wrapped spices in a large pot and add **2 quarts pale ale** and **2 cups honey**. Simmer on medium-low heat for about 20 minutes; remove from heat. To serve, pour **1 ounce dark rum** into a mug, then top with ale mixture. *Serves* about 10 to 12.

OLD FAITHFUL

In a large bowl, combine **1¼ cups powdered sugar**, **1 (750-ml) bottle bourbon**, and half of **1 (750-ml) bottle St.-Germain liqueur**. Whisk until sugar dissolves. Add **4 cups pink grapefruit juice**, **20 dashes grapefruit bitters**, about **30 mint leaves**, and **20 grapefruit peels**. Stir gently, then let sit for 1 hour before adding **1 (750-ml) bottle sparkling water**. Serve over ice. ***Serves*** *about 20.*

BRIGHT IDEA! If you can, pay for a cleaning service to come a few days before the party. That may sound extravagant, but it's money well spent.

COCKTAILS WORTH CELEBRATING

CHAMPAGNE COCKTAIL

Place **1 sugar cube** in a cocktail glass. Soak cube with **2 or 3 drops bitters**. Add **1 tablespoon cognac**. Pour in about **4 ounces chilled champagne** and garnish with **orange or lemon peel**, if desired. Serve immediately. *Makes* 1 drink.

SPARKLING WINTER SANGRIA
Shown on p. 188

In a medium bowl, combine **1 cup St.-Germain liqueur** and **½ cup superfine sugar**; whisk together until sugar dissolves. Add **¾ cup green grapes**, halved; **2 tangerines**, thinly sliced; and **½ small ruby red grapefruit**, quartered then thinly sliced; toss to combine. Refrigerate until chilled, 30 minutes or up to 3 hours. To serve, spoon some **fruit** and about **1 tablespoon liquid** into each glass. Divide **2 (750-ml) bottles chilled prosecco** among glasses. *Makes* 12 cocktails.

This Champagne Cocktail recipe is delicious whether it's made with great champagne, or budget brut.

CHEESY BITES

It takes just half an hour to pull together these delicious tidbits.

The retro Cheddar ball gets a delicious creamy upgrade from goat cheese.

GOAT CHEESE LOGS

Makes 2 cheese logs/16 servings
*Working time 15 min. **Total time** 25 min.*

- 2 logs (4-ounce) goat cheese
- 4 ounces cream cheese
- 3 teaspoons aged sweet sherry
- 1 teaspoon salt
- 1 teaspoon freshly ground black pepper
- 1½ teaspoons paprika
- ½ teaspoon cumin
- 4 teaspoons finely chopped fresh parsley
- 4 teaspoons finely chopped fresh dill

1. Stir goat cheese, cream cheese, sherry, salt, and pepper together in a small bowl. Wrap cheese mixture in plastic wrap and roll to shape into a log. Chill in freezer until slightly firm, about 10 minutes.
2. Meanwhile, mix paprika and cumin together in a small dish. Mix parsley and dill together in a separate small dish.
3. Remove goat cheese log from freezer, unwrap, and slice in half. Spread paprika-cumin mixture on 1 sheet of parchment paper and parsley-dill mixture on another sheet. Roll 1 log in paprika-cumin and 1 in parsley-dill. Serve with toasted pita and crostini.

SAVORY GRUYERE-APPLE TARTS

Makes 4 tarts Working time 10 min.
***Total time** 30 min.*

- 2 tablespoons unsalted butter
- 1 small yellow onion, finely diced
- 1 sheet frozen puff pastry, thawed
- 2 large Braeburn apples, peeled, cored, and thinly sliced
- 4 ounces Gruyère, chopped into ¼-inch cubes

1. Preheat oven to 400°F. In a small skillet over medium heat, melt 1 tablespoon butter. Sauté onion until softened, about 5 minutes. Set aside.
2. Meanwhile, on a work surface, roll out puff pastry to a 13- by 10-inch rectangle. Cut dough into four 6½- by 5-inch rectangles. Using a sharp knife, score 4 lines to create a ½-inch border all the way around each tart. Transfer to a parchment-lined baking pan.
3. Divide half of onion mixture among tarts. Layer apples in 3 slightly overlapping rows on each. Top with remaining onion mixture and cheese. Dot with remaining butter. Bake tarts until apples are tender and cheese is golden, about 20 minutes.

BRIGHT IDEA! Rather than spend big on a fancy centerpiece, arrange inexpensive herbs like rosemary and mint in silver mint julep cups, then line them down the center of the table.

Start with store-bought pizza dough for a quick and delicious party snack.

Just one teaspoon of chopped fresh rosemary lends explosive flavor to these quick-frying potato chips.

Sunchoke is a tasty and unusual alternative to potato in these chips.

CARAMELIZED LEEK AND BACON PIZZA

Makes 6 servings **Working time** *25 min.* **Total time** *40 min.*

- 6 slices thick-cut bacon, cut into ½-inch pieces
- 2 medium leeks, white and light green parts only, sliced
  Flour, for work surface
- 1 pound store-bought pizza dough
- 1 tablespoon olive oil
- ½ teaspoon garlic powder
- ¼ cup (about 2 ounces) mascarpone
- 1½ cup (about 6 ounces) shredded mozzarella
- ¼ cup (about 1 ounce) grated Parmesan

1. In a large pan over medium heat, cook bacon until crisp, about 8 minutes. Transfer to a paper-towel-lined plate; set aside. Drain all but a very thin layer of bacon fat from pan. Add leeks to pan and sauté until soft, about 12 minutes. Remove pan from heat; set aside.

2. Preheat oven, with pizza stone set on lowest rack, to 500°F. On a lightly floured surface and using a rolling pin, flatten dough to a 12-inch circle that's ½ inch thick. Drizzle crust with olive oil and sprinkle with garlic powder.

3. Using a rubber spatula, spread a thin layer of mascarpone on the crust. Sprinkle on half the mozzarella, then top with reserved leeks and bacon. Sprinkle on Parmesan and remaining mozzarella. Bake until crust is golden and cheese is bubbly, 10 to 12 minutes. Let sit 2 minutes before slicing.

SUNCHOKE CHIPS WITH WARM BLUE-CHEESE DIP

Makes 6 servings **Working time** *25 min.* **Total time** *40 min.*

- 1 cup plain Greek yogurt
- 4 tablespoons crumbled blue cheese
- 1 teaspoon freshly ground pepper
- 1 tablespoon salt
- 1½ teaspoon finely chopped fresh rosemary
- 2 pounds (large) sunchokes, well-scrubbed
  Vegetable oil
- 2 tablespoons chopped chives
  Dash freshly ground pepper

1. In a medium sauté pan over low heat, heat Greek yogurt, crumbled blue cheese, and 1 teaspoon freshly ground pepper for about 10 minutes, stirring well to combine. Keep warm. In a small bowl, toss salt and finely chopped fresh rosemary to combine; set aside. Thinly slice sunchokes. In a large sauté pan with a thermometer attached, over medium-high heat, heat 1 inch of vegetable oil until it reaches 375°F.

2. Working in batches, fry sunchokes until golden brown, 3 to 4 minutes. Transfer to a paper-towel-lined plate to drain, and immediately sprinkle hot chips with rosemary salt. Garnish warm blue-cheese dip with chopped chives and a dash more pepper, and serve alongside chips.

CRISPY ROSEMARY POTATO CHIPS

Makes 6 servings **Working time** *20 min.* **Total time** *20 min.*

- 2½ cups vegetable oil
- 1 pound russet potatoes, scrubbed and dried
- 1 teaspoon chopped fresh rosemary
  Sea salt
  Freshly ground pepper

1. In a medium saucepan fitted with a candy thermometer, heat oil to 325°F. Using a mandoline, slice potatoes widthwise into paper-thin slices.

2. In batches, fry potatoes in heated oil, 1 to 2 minutes, making sure not to overcrowd pan. Using a slotted spoon, transfer to a paper-towel-lined plate to drain. While still hot, sprinkle each batch with rosemary and salt and pepper to taste.

HAPPY HOLIDAY
HOR D'OEUVRES

LEMON GOAT-CHEESE DIP

Makes 12 servings *Working time* 10 min.
Total time 10 min.

1	cup mayonnaise
1	(10½-ounce) goat-cheese log, crumbled
2	tablespoon olive oil
2	green onions, chopped
1	tablespoon (about ½ lemon) fresh lemon juice
1	teaspoon (about ½ lemon) lemon zest
	Salt
	Freshly ground pepper
	Pita chips, for serving

In a food processor, combine first 6 ingredients, plus ½ teaspoon salt and 1 teaspoon pepper; blend until smooth. Transfer to a bowl and season with salt and pepper. Serve with pita chips.

DEVILED EGGS

Makes 12 eggs *Working time* 10 min.
Total time 20 min.

6	hard-boiled eggs
2	tablespoons finely chopped onion
2	tablespoons sweet relish
1	teaspoon dry mustard
½	teaspoon salt
¼	cup ranch dressing
	Paprika, for garnish
6	sprigs parsley, for garnish

1. Peel 6 hard-boiled eggs and cut into halves lengthwise. Remove yolks and place in a medium bowl; set whites aside on a platter. Mash yolks, using a fork, until fluffy. Mix in onion, sweet relish, dry mustard, salt, and ranch dressing until smooth.
2. Fill a large, sealable plastic bag with yolk mixture. Cut corner of bag to create a ¾-inch hole and pipe filling into well of each egg white. Chill until ready to serve. Garnish with a sprinkle of paprika and a sprig of parsley.

BACON DIP

Makes 2 cups *Working time* 20 min.
Total time 50 min.

½	pound bacon
3	small scallions, thinly sliced
3	sun-dried tomatoes, finely chopped
4	ounces softened cream cheese
⅔	cup ranch dressing

1. Cook bacon until crisp. Drain on paper towels, then finely chop. Reserve 2 tablespoons chopped bacon and stir rest together in a medium bowl with scallions, sun-dried tomatoes, cream cheese, and ranch dressing.
2. Transfer to a serving dish and chill for 30 minutes. Garnish with reserved bacon and additional sliced scallions. Serve with fresh vegetables or crackers.

For a more calorie-conscious concoction, substitute low-fat Greek yogurt for mayo in Lemon Goat-Cheese Dip.

Ranch dressing is the secret ingredient in this creamy Bacon Dip.

Christmas carolers deserve a cup of hot chocolate—brimming with marshmallows!

A JOYOUS CAROLING PARTY

After a night spent singing in brisk winter air, carolers have earned mugs of steaming hot chocolate and tasty sweet treats. The same recipes would be perfectly at home at other wintertime activities—a sledding party, or après cross-country skiing, for example.

SELF-SERVE HOT CHOCOLATE BAR

Whip up two kinds of cocoa—one dark, one pale—both irresistible. For each variation (each makes 8 servings), bring 7 cups of milk to a simmer in a medium pan over low heat, then whisk in the ingredients that follow.

Classic Hot Chocolate

1   pound bittersweet chocolate, chopped
1   cup heavy cream
1   cup sugar
2   teaspoons vanilla extract

Winter-White Hot Chocolate

1   pound white chocolate, chopped
1   cup heavy cream
2   teaspoons vanilla extract
   Sugar, to taste

Set out a sweet garnish station. Let guests customized their own drinks with ginger candies, crushed Butterfingers, coconut flakes, mini marshmallows, sliced Kit Kats, and caramel syrup. Chocolate-dipped biscuit sticks and peppermint sticks function as stirrers.

POPCORN, S'MORES, HOT CHOCOLATE— YUM!

Conjure up a little snow business: Decanters of dark rum and vanilla vodka sit atop a snowflake-bedecked tablecloth (which is simple to make using stencils and white fabric paint).

Dark Rum

Vanilla Vodka

The secret to this salty-sweet snack is ready-made caramel syrup, melted and drizzled over popcorn.

Festive meringue snowflakes are created from just four ingredients!

MERINGUE SNOWFLAKES

Makes 12–16 snowflakes **Working time** 35 min. **Total time** 3 hr. 15 min.

- 3   large eggs, separated
- ½   teaspoon cream of tartar
        Salt
- ¾   cup superfine sugar
        Dragées, optional

1. Place egg whites in a medium bowl and let stand for 30 minutes; discard yolks.

2. Add cream of tartar and a pinch of salt. Using an electric mixer set on medium, beat until soft peaks form. Increase speed to high and add sugar, 1 tablespoon at a time, beating until stiff peaks form and sugar is nearly dissolved.

3. Preheat oven to 300°F. Meanwhile, pour meringue mixture into a pastry bag fitted with a large (⅜-inch) star-shaped tip. Using the photo as a guide, pipe 3-inch-diameter snowflake shapes onto two parchment-lined baking sheets. Decorate the tops with dragées, if desired. Bake for 10 minutes, then turn off oven. Let meringues dry in oven, with door closed, for 1 hour.

4. Carefully peel meringues from parchment and transfer to a wire rack to cool completely, about 20 minutes.

Pulled Pork
p. 205

A HOLIDAY BUFFET ON A BUDGET

Yes, Virginia, you can host an amazing bash without breaking the bank. The easy-to-make menu on the following pages feeds 20, and covers soup to nuts, plus some seriously hearty pulled pork and swanky signature cocktails.

Cabbage Slaw
p. 205

Onion and Cilantro Garnish
p. 205

Mini-Biscuits
p. 205

BRIGHT IDEA! Scatter tea lights everywhere to make a room glow. They don't cost much but look magical.

Pigs in Blankets
p. 207

Roasted Winter Squash Soup
p. 205

Get out your slow cooker and whip up these spectacular sandwiches.

Ten minutes is all it takes to create this special popcorn.

BRIGHT IDEA! Simplify your buffet prep by sticking Post-It notes on empty platters and bowls, indicating which finished dish goes where.

Skip the bowls and serve this creamy squash soup in pretty juice glasses.

DOWN HOME & DELICIOUS

ROASTED WINTER SQUASH SOUP

Makes 20 servings/16 cups *Working time* 10 min. *Total time* 1 hr. 10 min.

- 8 pounds butternut squash, peeled, seeded, and cut into 1-inch cubes
- 2 large onions, chopped
- 6 cloves garlic, minced
- 3 tablespoons curry powder
- 1 teaspoon salt
- ¾ teaspoon freshly ground pepper
- 6 tablespoons vegetable oil
- 8 cups low-sodium vegetable broth
   Sour cream, for garnish

1. Preheat oven to 400°F. In a large bowl, toss butternut squash, onions, garlic, curry powder, salt, and pepper with vegetable oil to coat. Divide between 2 baking pans and roast until browned, 45 minutes.
2. Using a blender, puree batches of roasted vegetables with vegetable broth.
3. Transfer to a large pot and heat. Serve warm with a dollop of sour cream.

SMOKY POPCORN

Makes 20 cups *Working time* 10 min. *Total time* 10 min.

In a large pot, pop **1 cup corn kernels** in **¼ cup vegetable oil**. Transfer popcorn to a large bowl, drizzle with **¼ cup vegetable oil**, then toss with **⅔ cup finely aged Gouda, 1 tablespoon smoked paprika,** and **2 teaspoons salt**.

PULLED PORK & BISCUITS, PLUS GARNISHES AND SLAW

Makes 20 servings/8 cups pork; 40 mini-biscuits; 4 cups cabbage slaw *Working time* 20 min. *Total time* 6 hr. 30 min.

PORK
- 7 pounds pork shoulder roast
- 3 tablespoons chili powder
- 1½ teaspoons salt
- 1 teaspoon freshly ground pepper
- 1 large onion, sliced
- 4 cloves garlic, minced
- 3 cups barbecue sauce, divided
- 4 cups water

MINI BISCUITS
- 5 cups all-purpose flour
- 2 tablespoons baking powder
- 1½ teaspoons salt
- 2 sticks unsalted butter
- 2½ cups buttermilk

GARNISHES
- 1 bag (14 ounces) cabbage slaw
- 1 cup apple-cider vinegar
- 1 medium red onion
- 1 bunch fresh cilantro

1. Trim pork shoulder roast of any excess skin and fat. In a small bowl, combine chili powder, salt, and pepper and rub mixture all over pork roast until thoroughly coated. Place onion and garlic in bottom of a 4- to 6-quart slow cooker, then add roast and 1 cup barbecue sauce (such as KC Masterpiece). Pour water over roast until covered.

2. Cover slow cooker and cook pork on high until very tender and meat falls off bone, about 6 hours. Carefully remove pork from slow cooker and reserve on a platter. Strain cooking liquid into sink, reserving onion; return pork and onion to slow cooker; shred meat with a fork and add 2 more cups barbecue sauce. Cook on high until heated, about 8 minutes.
3. To make mini biscuits, preheat oven to 450°F. In a large bowl, stir flour, baking powder, and 1½ teaspoons salt. Using a pastry blender, cut in butter until mixture resembles coarse meal. Using a fork, stir in buttermilk just until dough forms. Knead 3 to 4 turns on a lightly floured surface and divide into 2 equal balls dough. Pat 1 ball dough into ½-inch-thick disk and cut out biscuits using a 2-inch cutter (gathering and incorporating scraps until all dough has been used). Repeat with remaining ball dough. Place biscuits 1 inch apart on parchment-lined baking sheets. Bake until golden and fluffy, about 15 minutes. Transfer to a wire rack to cool.
4. Meanwhile, prepare garnishes: In a small bowl, toss cabbage slaw with apple-cider vinegar; set aside. Thinly slice red onion, then remove leaves from cilantro; set aside.
5. To assemble sandwiches, split mini biscuits with a fork and top each with about 3 tablespoons pork. Garnish with slaw or cilantro and red onion, if desired.

Serve up
Mini Bread
Puddings for
a delectable
dessert.

Pigs in Blankets
are as close to a
universal favorite
as it gets.

IRRESISTIBLE PARTY TREATS!

PIGS IN BLANKETS

Makes 20 servings/60 pieces **Working time** 15 min. **Total time** 40 min.

1. Preheat oven to 425°F. On a lightly floured surface, roll **1 sheet thawed frozen puff pastry dough** into a 12- by 14-inch rectangle. Cut rectangle in half lengthwise, then cut each half into 3 equal pieces for a total of 6 pastry pieces. Repeat with second pastry.
2. Pat **12 all-beef hot dogs** dry with paper towels and pierce each several times with a fork. In a small bowl, whisk together **1 large egg** and **¼ teaspoon salt** for egg wash. Roll each hot dog in 1 puff pastry piece, then seal with some egg wash.
3. Place pastry-wrapped hot dogs on parchment-lined baking sheets and lightly brush with remaining egg wash; sprinkle with **poppy seeds**. Bake until puffed and golden, about 20 minutes. Slice each pastry-wrapped hot dog into 5 sections and serve warm with **spicy mustard**, if desired.

MINI BREAD PUDDINGS

Makes 20 servings **Working time** 20 min. **Total time** 2 hr.

12 slices white bread
1⅓ cups semisweet chocolate chips
10 large eggs
1 cup sugar
1 teaspoon vanilla extract
¼ teaspoon salt
1½ cups whole milk
1½ cups heavy cream
   Whipped cream (optional)
   Crushed peppermints (optional)

1. Preheat oven to 350°F. Toast bread on 2 baking sheets until slices are dry but not brown, about 15 minutes, flipping after 7 minutes. Cool completely on sheet.
2. Meanwhile, line 20 cups in 2 standard-size muffin tins with paper liners. Cut cooled toast into ½-inch cubes and divide, along with chocolate chips, among muffin cups. Gently shake tins to distribute chips evenly; set aside.
3. In a large bowl, whisk eggs, sugar, vanilla extract, and salt until sugar is dissolved. Add milk and heavy cream and continue whisking until smooth. Pour custard evenly over bread cubes and chocolate chips in muffin cups. Let stand until bread absorbs custard, about 20 minutes.
4. Place muffin tins on pans with 1-inch sides. Pour water into pans, creating a bath around muffin tins. Bake until custard sets and tops are golden, 45 to 50 minutes. Cool in muffin tins on a wire rack.
5. Serve with whipped cream and crushed peppermints, if desired.

DRINKS & NUTS: DIVINE DETAILS

SPICY ROSEMARY PEANUTS

Makes 20 servings/8 cups
Working time 5 min.
Total time 13 min.

1. Preheat oven to 375°F. Line 2 baking sheets with parchment paper and spread out **2 pounds unsalted dry-roasted peanuts** in an even layer. Toast in oven until golden, about 8 minutes.
2. Meanwhile, in a large bowl, combine **¼ stick melted unsalted butter**, **3 tablespoons finely chopped fresh rosemary, 1 ½ teaspoons garlic powder, 1 ½ teaspoons salt**, and **¾ teaspoon cayenne pepper**. Add hot peanuts to bowl and toss with butter-herb mixture until thoroughly coated.

THE COCKTAILS

Warm Bourbon Cider

Makes 20 servings
Working time 10 min.

In a stockpot, heat **1 gallon (16 cups) fresh apple cider, 5 teaspoons ground cinnamon**, and **2½ teaspoons each ground nutmeg and ground ginger**. When mixture is hot but not boiling, remove from heat and add **3 cups bourbon**. (**Note:** One 1.75-liter bottle yields enough liquor for both this recipe and the punch below.) Stir to distribute spices and divide cider among 20 mugs.

Tropical Bourbon Punch

Makes 20 servings
Working time 10 min.

In a large container, whisk together **6 cups ruby-red grapefruit juice, 2 cups pineapple juice, ½ cup honey**, and **4 cups bourbon** until combined. Before guests arrive, pour mixture into a punch bowl and gently stir in **2 cups cold seltzer water**.

Cranberry Cava Cocktails

Makes 20 servings
Working time 10 min., plus chilling

In a small saucepan over medium heat, combine **1 cup each sugar and water**, stirring until sugar dissolves. Remove from heat, then add **1 cup halved fresh cranberries** and **1½ teaspoons vanilla extract**; refrigerate at least 12 hours. To mix cocktail, add to each flute **1 tablespoon of the cranberry simple syrup**, plus **4 cranberries** from syrup, then top with a **sparkling cava**. (**Note:** You'll need four 750-milliliter bottles.)

Guaranteed to produce a holiday glow: Spicy Rosemary Peanuts and Warm Bourbon Cider.

BRIGHT IDEA! It's smart to pick up three or four extra bags of ice before your party.

Two of the drinks on this streamlined bar rely on bourbon for their kick; the sparkling wine can be enjoyed straight up or with a dash of cranberry syrup.

Nothing brightens up a winter morning like a vibrant salad of grapefruit, lime, and navel and blood oranges.

MAPLE-CITRUS SALAD WITH COCONUT

Makes 8 servings *Working time* 15 *min.* *Total time* 15 min.

- 2 large pink grapefruits, peel and pith removed
- 2 large navel oranges, peel and pith removed
- 2 blood oranges, peel and pith removed
- 1 lime, peel and pith removed
- 1½ tablespoons pure maple syrup
- 6 tablespoons fresh coconut shavings
- 2 tablespoons fresh tarragon, for garnish

1. Set a fine-mesh sieve over a medium bowl. Slice in between membranes of grapefruits and 1 navel orange to release segments into sieve; transfer segments to a large platter. Squeeze any remaining juice from citrus membranes into sieve. Set aside bowl with juice. Slice remaining navel orange, blood oranges, and lime crosswise into ¼-inch-thick rounds and layer atop grapefruit and orange segments on platter.

2. In a small bowl, combine ½ cup reserved juice with maple syrup. Pour syrup mixture over citrus. (Citrus can be stored, covered, in a refrigerator for up to 1 day.) Sprinkle coconut over citrus and gently toss. Garnish with tarragon before serving.

A CELEBRATORY BRUNCH

Inviting family and friends for a mid-morning brunch is a low-stress (and budget-conscious) way to entertain during the holidays, or any time of year. And the appealing fare on these pages is well worth getting up for!

Standard mimosas get an upgrade with the addition of raspberry and peach purees.

You can assemble this egg casserole—loaded with French bread, tomatoes, and broccoli—the night before.

LIKE BREAKFAST, ONLY BETTER!

TOMATO-CHEDDAR STRATA WITH BROCCOLI

Makes 8 servings **Working time** 15 min.
Total time 2 hr. 15 min.

4½ cups (about ¾ of a French loaf) 1-inch bread cubes

Butter, for greasing dish

6 ounces shredded Cheddar (about 1½ cups)

1 cup halved grape tomatoes

1 cup frozen broccoli florets

1½ tablespoons chopped fresh Italian parsley

8 large eggs

3 cups milk

1¼ teaspoons salt

⅛ teaspoons freshly ground pepper

4 ounces (½ cup) ricotta cheese

1 teaspoon herbes de Provence

1. Place bread in a buttered 9- by 13-inch baking dish. Top bread with 1 cup Cheddar, tomatoes, broccoli, and 1 tablespoon parsley.

2. In a large bowl, whisk together eggs, milk, salt, and pepper. Pour egg mixture over bread and gently press to soak every cube. Add dollops of ricotta over top. Sprinkle strata with herbes de Provence and remaining Cheddar. Cover and refrigerate for several hours or up to overnight.

3. Remove strata from refrigerator and bring to room temperature, about 1 hour. Meanwhile, preheat oven to 350°F. Bake until strata is puffed and lightly golden brown, about 1 hour. Set aside to cool for 10 minutes. Garnish with remaining parsley. Serve warm or at room temperature.

PEACH MELBA MIMOSAS

Makes 8 cocktails **Working time** 10 min.
Total time 10 min.

1½ cups thawed frozen raspberries

¼ cup sugar

1 cup thawed frozen peaches

1 teaspoon fresh lemon juice

2 bottles chilled champagne, cava, or other sparkling white wine

½ pint fresh raspberries, for garnish

1. In a blender, puree frozen raspberries and 2 tablespoons sugar. Set a fine sieve over a small pitcher and strain puree; set aside.

2. Rinse blender, then puree peaches with remaining sugar, lemon juice, and 3 tablespoons cold water.

3. Spoon 2 teaspoons raspberry puree and 2 teaspoons peach puree into each glass. Top off each cocktail with champagne and garnish with fresh raspberries. Serve warm or at room temperature.

SWEET & SAVORY DELIGHTS

GRAPEFRUIT BUTTERMILK DOUGHNUTS WITH CANDIED ZEST

Makes 12 doughnuts *Working time* 20 min.
Total time 1 hr.

Nonstick cooking spray
2 cups all-purpose flour
2 cups granulated sugar
2 teaspoons baking powder
1 teaspoon ground ginger
½ teaspoon salt
1¼ cups buttermilk
1 large egg
2 tablespoons canola oil
1 teaspoon vanilla extract
1 large grapefruit, zested
4 strips (each 2 inches long) grapefruit zest, thinly sliced
1 cup confectioners' sugar
3 tablespoons grapefruit juice

1. Coat two 6-cavity doughnut pans with nonstick spray. Preheat oven to 350°F. Meanwhile, in a large bowl, combine flour, 1½ cups granulated sugar, baking powder, ginger, and salt, and mix well. In a small bowl, whisk buttermilk, egg, canola oil, vanilla, and zest of 1 grapefruit to combine. Add wet ingredients to dry ingredients and stir. Spoon the batter into the prepared pans, filling each cavity a little more than ¾ full. Bake for 25 to 30 minutes. Let cool in pan for 5 minutes, then turn doughnuts out onto a wire rack to cool completely.
2. In a small bowl, whisk confectioners' sugar and juice until smooth. Set glaze aside. In a small saucepan, combine zest strips, 3 tablespoons granulated sugar, and 3 tablespoons water, and bring to a boil. Reduce heat to low and simmer mixture until sugar dissolves, about 5 minutes. Strain. Toss zest immediately in remaining granulated sugar until coated. Transfer to a cutting board and chop.
3. For each doughnut, carefully dip the top in glaze, then set on a wire rack, glaze side up, so excess drips off. Sprinkle immediately with chopped zest.

MAPLE-SAGE PORK SAUSAGE

Makes 10 patties *Working time* 15 min.
Total time 30 min.

2 pounds coarsely ground pork
6 tablespoons pure maple syrup
¼ cup finely chopped fresh Italian parsley
2 tablespoons finely chopped fresh sage
2 teaspoons salt
¼ teaspoon freshly ground pepper
¼ teaspoon ground nutmeg
¼ cup vegetable oil

1. Preheat oven to 175 °F. Place a sheet pan in oven. In a large bowl, mix together all ingredients, except oil, until combined. Form mixture into sixteen 2-inch-round patties. (Patties can be stored, covered, in a refrigerator for up to 1 day.)
2. In a large skillet over medium-high heat, heat oil. Working in batches, cook patties until browned, about 3 minutes per side. Transfer to a paper-towel-lined plate. Transfer sausage to sheet pan in oven and cover loosely with foil while cooking remaining patties.

This appealing spread—rack of lamb, fennel salad, onion pie, and more—gives reason to rejoice. (Recipes on pages 244, 229, and 238.)

Starters, Entrées, and Sides: Best-Ever Holiday Dinner Recipes

Christmas dinner is a little bit free-form. For Thanksgiving, you know you're going to serve turkey. A big bird works well on December 25th, too, but so do a whole host of other entrées—so you can choose a new favorite tradition, or try something different every year. We've collected **Country Living**'s favorite holiday recipes and wrapped them up here for you. Open and enjoy for years to come!

ALL-TIME GREATEST HOLIDAY RECIPES

From roast turkey and stuffings to salads, green beans, and other sides, these dishes from *Country Living's* kitchens have more than stood the test of time.

BRIGHT IDEA! For a fresh garnish that won't wilt, choose stiff, glossy leaves. Here, bay and citrus leaves pair with figs and kumquats.

THE PERFECT ROAST TURKEY

Makes 8 servings **Working time** *20 min.*
Total time *4 hr.*

1   (13 to 15-pound) fresh or thawed
    frozen turkey (neck and giblets
    removed)
    Salt and freshly ground pepper
1   medium onion, cut into quarters
1   large carrot, cut into thirds
4   tablespoons unsalted butter,
    melted

1. Preheat oven to 325°F. Rinse turkey with cold water, drain well, and pat dry with paper towels. Season inside the cavity with 1 teaspoon salt and ½ teaspoon pepper. Stuff cavity with onion and carrot, and tie legs together using butcher's twine.

2. In a roasting pan fitted with a rack, place turkey breast-side up. Rub butter under and over skin. Rub skin with 1 teaspoon each salt and pepper. Loosely tent turkey with heavy-duty aluminum foil.

3. Roast turkey for 1 hour, then baste with pan juices. Roast for 1 more hour, then remove and discard foil and baste. Continue roasting, basting turkey every 30 minutes, until an instant-read thermometer reaches 170°F when inserted into thickest part of thigh, 3½ to 4 hours total.

4. Let turkey rest for 20 minutes, cut off butcher's twine, and remove carrot and onion from cavity and discard. Drain any juices from cavity into roasting pan and transfer turkey to a serving platter. Serve with gravy. (For the best way to make gravy, see sidebar at right.)

TWO TASTY TWISTS

1. If you have time, consider brining your bird overnight to ensure juicy meat infused with subtle flavor.

2. Spice up The Perfect Roast Turkey with a zesty rub. Our Herbes de Provence Turkey calls for ½ cup dried lavender; 1 tablespoon each salt, fennel seeds, and dried thyme; and 2 teaspoons white peppercorns. Just pulse in a spice grinder until the mixture is fine but not powdery. Then, at Step 2 in the recipe at left, omit the butter. And instead of salt and pepper, work the spice rub under and over the turkey's skin.

THE BEST WAY TO MAKE GRAVY

1. Remove turkey from roasting pan. Pour drippings into a fat separator. Once fat rises to the top, pour turkey juices into a 4-cup measuring cup; add enough chicken broth to equal 4 cups total. Set aside. Reserve fat in separator.

2. In a large skillet over medium heat, slowly add ½ cup flour to ¼ cup reserved turkey fat, whisking constantly. Cook, continuing to whisk, until roux is sizzling and golden brown, about 5 minutes.

3. Gradually add turkey-juice and broth mixture to roux. Cook, whisking constantly to dissolve lumps, until gravy thickens, 8 to 9 minutes. Reduce heat to medium-low and simmer for about 5 minutes. Season with salt and pepper.

Wild Rice and Basmati Dressing with Sausage and Sage

The Fabulous Beekman Boys' Cornbread Stuffing with Pecans and Sweet Sausage

Edythe Newman's Matzo Stuffing

Sourdough and Mushroom Stuffing

WILD RICE AND BASMATI DRESSING WITH SAUSAGE AND SAGE

Makes 8 servings **Working time** *30 min.*
Total time *1 hr. 50 min.*

- 1 pound bulk pork sausage
- 2 tablespoons unsalted butter, plus more for casserole dish
- 1 large Spanish onion, chopped
- ¼ pound small mushrooms (such as white button), sliced
- ⅔ cup wild rice, rinsed and drained
- 4 cups low-sodium chicken broth
- 2 tablespoons chopped fresh sage
- 2 bay leaves
- ⅔ cup basmati rice
- ¼ cup chopped fresh parsley
  Salt and freshly ground pepper

1. In a large pot over medium heat, cook sausage, breaking up with a wooden spoon, until browned and fat is rendered, about 10 minutes. Using a slotted spoon, transfer sausage to a plate; set aside. Discard fat and wipe pan clean.

2. In same pot over medium heat, melt butter. Add onion and cook until soft, about 10 minutes. Add mushrooms and cook until soft, about 8 minutes. Stir in wild rice. Add broth, sage, and bay leaves. Increase heat to high and bring to a boil. Reduce heat to low, cover, and cook for 25 minutes. Stir in basmati rice, cover, and continue to cook until both rices are tender, about 20 minutes. Remove from heat, discard bay leaves, and stir in reserved sausage, parsley, 1½ teaspoons salt, and 1 teaspoon pepper.

3. Preheat oven to 350°F. Allow rice mixture to rest in pot while oven preheats. Transfer to a buttered 3-quart casserole dish and bake until hot and browned on top, about 20 minutes.

THE FABULOUS BEEKMAN BOYS' CORNBREAD STUFFING WITH PECANS AND SWEET SAUSAGE

Makes 8 servings **Working time** 20 min.
Total time 1 hr. 10 min.

- ¾ tablespoon extra-virgin olive oil
- 1 large onion, coarsely chopped
- ¾ pound sweet Italian sausage (without fennel seeds), casings removed
- 3 ounces pecans (about ¾ cup), toasted
- ½ cup chopped fresh parsley
  Zest of 1 lemon (about 1 tablespoon)
- 5-6 cups cubed, day-old corn bread, cut into 1-inch chunks
- 1 cup plus 2 tablespoons low-sodium chicken broth
- 6 tablespoons unsalted butter, melted
  Salt and freshly ground pepper

1. Preheat oven to 350°F. In a large skillet, heat oil over medium heat. Add onion and cook until tender, about 7 minutes. Add sausage and cook, breaking up with a wooden spoon, until browned, 5 to 7 minutes. Using a slotted spoon, transfer mixture to a large bowl.
2. Add pecans, parsley, zest, and cornbread to bowl and toss to combine. Add broth, butter, 1 teaspoon salt, and ½ teaspoon pepper and toss until moistened. Transfer to a 3-quart casserole dish, cover with a piece of aluminum foil, and bake for 20 minutes. Remove foil and bake until hot and browned on top, about 15 minutes more.

EDYTHE NEWMAN'S MATZO STUFFING

Makes 8 servings **Working time** 20 min.
Total time 1 hr. 35 min.

- 2 large onions, coarsely chopped
- 2 large Gala apples, peeled, cored, and coarsely chopped
- 3 stalks celery, chopped
- ½ cup olive oil, plus more for casserole dish
- 2 large eggs, lightly beaten
- 1 tablespoon ground cinnamon
- 2 teaspoons poultry seasoning (preferably Bell's)
  Salt
- 1 (12-ounce) box matzo meal
- 2 cups low-sodium chicken broth

1. Preheat oven to 350°F. In a large bowl, combine first 7 ingredients plus 1 teaspoon salt.
2. Add ⅓ matzo meal and 1 cup broth, stirring to mix. Add another ⅓ of meal and ½ cup broth; stir again. Repeat with remaining meal and broth. Stir until mixture is combined and has a moist, stuffing-like consistency.
3. Transfer to an oiled 3-quart casserole dish, cover with a piece of oiled aluminum foil, and bake for 45 minutes. Remove foil and bake until hot and browned on top, about 30 minutes more.

SOURDOUGH AND MUSHROOM STUFFING

Makes 8 servings **Working time** 15 min.
Total time 1 hr. 30 min.

- 2 tablespoons unsalted butter, plus more for casserole dish
- 1 pound assorted mushrooms (such as shiitake, oyster, and cremini), sliced
- 9 stalks celery, chopped
- 2 medium onions, finely chopped
  Salt and freshly ground pepper
- 1 (1-pound) loaf sourdough bread, cut into 1-inch cubes
- 1½ cups low-sodium chicken broth
- ½ cup chopped fresh flat-leaf parsley
- 1 tablespoon chopped fresh thyme
- 1 tablespoon chopped fresh sage
- 1 teaspoon chopped fresh rosemary

1. Preheat oven to 350°F. In a large pot over medium-high heat, melt butter. Add mushrooms and cook until soft, about 10 minutes. Add celery and onions, and cook until soft, about 10 minutes. Remove from heat. Add 2 teaspoons salt, 1 teaspoon pepper, and remaining ingredients; toss to combine.
2. Transfer to a buttered 3-quart casserole dish, cover with a piece of aluminum foil, and bake for 45 minutes. Remove foil and bake until hot and browned on top, about 20 minutes more.

CRACKED-PEPPER DINNER ROLLS

Makes 16 rolls *Working time* 30 min.
Total time 1 hr. 45 min.

- 3⅓ cups all-purpose flour; plus more for kneading, if necessary
- 4 teaspoons rapid-rise dry yeast (from 2 packets)
- 2 teaspoons sugar
  Salt and freshly ground pepper
- 2 large eggs (1 separated)
- 4 teaspoons butter, melted; plus more for pan

1. In a large bowl, combine 2⅔ cups flour, yeast, sugar, ¾ teaspoon salt, and 2 teaspoons pepper.

2. In a medium bowl, whisk together 1 egg and 1 egg white. Whisk in ⅔ cup warm water (120°F to 130°F) and butter. Using a wooden spoon, stir egg mixture into flour mixture until a soft dough forms.

3. Sprinkle ⅓ cup flour onto a work surface. Transfer dough to surface. Sprinkle dough with remaining flour and knead until smooth and elastic, about 5 minutes. (If sticky, add another 2 to 3 tablespoons flour.) Pat dough into a ball. Place in a large bowl, cover with a clean towel, and let rise, about 20 minutes.

4. Punch down dough. Divide into 16 equal portions, forming each into a ball (about 1¾ inches in diameter). Transfer balls into a buttered 16-muffin pan. Cover with lightly buttered plastic wrap and let dough rise until doubled in size, about 30 minutes.

5. Preheat oven to 350°F. In a small bowl, beat 1½ teaspoons water and remaining egg yolk. Brush tops of rolls with half the egg wash. Bake until golden brown and rolls sound hollow when tapped, 20 to 25 minutes. Brush tops with remaining egg wash. Return pan to oven and bake for 5 minutes more. Transfer rolls to a wire rack to cool.

RUBY RED GRAPEFRUIT AND CHICORY SALAD

Makes 8 servings *Working time* 20 min.
Total time 50 min.

- 3 large ruby red grapefruits
- ½ cup olive oil
- 3 tablespoons red-wine vinegar
- ½ teaspoon ground cumin
  Salt and freshly ground pepper
- 1 head chicory, torn into bite-size pieces
- 1 small red onion, sliced into rings

1. Using a serrated knife, slice away peel and pith of each grapefruit. Working over a bowl to catch and reserve juices, segment grapefruits by slicing along membranes; place segments in same bowl. Transfer 3 tablespoons grapefruit juice to a pint-size jar; set aside. Cover bowl with plastic wrap and refrigerate for 30 minutes or up to 4 hours.

2. Meanwhile, add oil, vinegar, cumin, and ½ teaspoon salt to jar. Seal jar and shake until mixed. Refrigerate until ready to serve or up to 4 hours.

3. Place chicory, onion, and reserved grapefruit segments in a serving bowl. Drizzle dressing over salad. Season with salt and pepper. Toss to combine.

BRIGHT IDEA! To segment a grapefruit, first cut off the top and bottom. Slice away the peel and pith, then slice along the membranes to release the segments.

Ruby Red Grapefruit and Chicory Salad

Cracked-Pepper Dinner Rolls

ALL-TIME GREATEST HOLIDAY RECIPES

Potato and Celery Root Gratin with Gouda

BRIGHT IDEA! Use a mandoline to slice potatoes uniformly and paper thin!

Marvin Woods's Brussels Sprouts, Red Pepper, and Avocado Salad

Green Beans with Bacon
recipe on
p.226

Light and Fluffy Carrot Soufflés

LIGHT AND FLUFFY CARROT SOUFFLÉS

Makes 8 soufflés *Working time* 30 min. *Total time* 1 hr. 40 min.

8   medium carrots, chopped
4   tablespoons unsalted butter, plus more for ramekins
1   small onion, finely chopped
¼   cup all-purpose flour
¼   teaspoon freshly grated nutmeg
      Salt and freshly ground pepper
1⅓   cups whole milk
8   large eggs, separated

1. In a medium pot over high heat, bring 2 inches water to a boil. Add carrots and cook until tender, about 15 minutes. Drain, reserving cooking water. Puree carrots in a food processor until smooth. If needed, add 2 to 3 tablespoons cooking water; puree should measure 1 to 1¼ cups. Discard remaining cooking water.

2. In same pot over medium-high heat, melt butter. Add onion and cook until tender, about 5 minutes. Stir in flour, nutmeg, 1 teaspoon salt, and ¼ teaspoon pepper. Remove pot from heat. While stirring, gradually add milk. Return pot to medium-high and bring to a boil, stirring constantly, until mixture is smooth and thickened, about 3 minutes. Stir in carrot puree and set aside to cool to room temperature.

3. Preheat oven to 350°F. Meanwhile, butter eight ¾-cup ramekins; set on a baking pan.

4. In a medium bowl and using an electric beater, beat egg yolks until pale, about 3 minutes. Stir yolks into carrot mixture. In another bowl and using a whisk, beat egg whites to stiff peaks. Add 1½ cups egg whites to carrot mixture and stir to combine. Using a rubber spatula, gently fold remaining egg whites into carrot mixture.

5. Divide mixture among ramekins and bake until soufflés puff up, 20 to 25 minutes— do not open oven during baking.

MARVIN WOODS'S BRUSSELS SPROUTS, RED PEPPER, AND AVOCADO SALAD

Makes 8 servings *Working time* 10 min. *Total time* 20 min.

1   pound Brussels sprouts, trimmed
1   cup naval orange juice (about 3 navel oranges)
½   cup grapeseed oil
½   cup white balsamic vinegar
2   tablespoons agave syrup
2   small red onions, thinly sliced
¼   cup chopped fresh cilantro
½   jalapeño, seeded and thinly sliced
1   avocado, diced
2   roasted red peppers, diced
      Salt and freshly ground pepper

1. Bring a large pot of water to a boil over high heat. Meanwhile, remove outer leaves of Brussels sprouts and discard cores. Fill a bowl with ice water. Blanch leaves in boiling water until bright green, about 40 seconds. Remove with a slotted spoon, then plunge into ice water until cool, 15 to 30 seconds. Drain leaves on paper towels and blot dry.

2. In a medium bowl, whisk together next 7 ingredients.

3. Place leaves, avocado, and red peppers in a serving dish. Drizzle dressing over salad. Season with salt and pepper. Toss to combine.

POTATO AND CELERY ROOT GRATIN WITH GOUDA

Makes 8 servings *Working time* 40 min. *Total time* 1 hr. 40 min.

1¼   cups heavy cream
¼   cup whole milk
1   small onion, halved
2   large garlic cloves, smashed
      Butter, for casserole dish
1   pound celery root
1½   pounds Yukon gold potatoes
      Salt and freshly ground pepper
2   ounces aged Gouda, grated (about ½ cup)

1. Preheat oven to 400°F. In a medium pan over medium-high heat, bring heavy cream, milk, onion, and garlic to a boil. Remove from heat; steep for about 30 minutes.

2. Meanwhile, using a sharp knife, peel, halve, and thinly slice celery root; cut slices in half. Peel and thinly slice potatoes. In a buttered 8-inch casserole dish, arrange a layer of celery-root slices followed by a layer of potato slices. Season with salt and pepper. Repeat.

3. Remove onion and garlic from cream mixture and discard. Pour mixture over casserole. Cover dish with a piece of buttered aluminum foil and bake for 40 minutes.

4. Remove foil and sprinkle casserole with Gouda. Bake until bubbly and golden, about 15 minutes. Transfer casserole to a wire rack and allow to rest 15 minutes before serving.

GREEN BEANS WITH BACON

Makes 8 servings **Working time** *25 min.*
Total time *45 min.*

Salt and freshly ground pepper
2¼ pounds fresh green beans
4 slices bacon, chopped
2 medium shallots, chopped
¼ cup chopped pecans
(about 1 ounce)
6 tablespoons white-wine vinegar
1½ tablespoons sugar

1. In a large pot over high heat, bring 2½ quarts salted water to a boil. Working in batches, add green beans and cook 2 minutes per batch. Transfer to a bowl. Set aside.
2. In a large pan over medium heat, cook bacon until crisp, about 7 minutes. Transfer to a paper-towel-lined plate; set aside. Sauté shallots for 2 minutes; add pecans and cook for 1 minute. Remove pan from heat; add vinegar and sugar, stirring until sugar dissolves.
3. Add reserved green beans to pan; cook over low heat until heated through, about 4 minutes. Season with salt and pepper. Transfer to a dish; top with reserved bacon.

TASTY TIP

Make bacon even better by using candied bacon with these green beans. Preheat oven to 400°F. Line a baking pan with aluminum foil and fit with a rack. Toss 4 slices bacon with 2 tablespoons dark brown sugar to coat. Cook bacon until shiny and crisp, 15 to 20 minutes. Let bacon cool, then chop and sprinkle on beans in Step 3 of recipe above.

CREAMED KALE GRATIN

Makes 8 servings **Working time** *30 min.*
Total time *1 hr. 30 min.*

4 bunches of kale (about 1 ¾ pounds), washed and thick stems removed
1½ large Vidalia onions (about 1 ¼ pounds), thinly sliced
6 tablespoons butter
1¼ teaspoons salt
¾ teaspoon freshly ground pepper
5 teaspoons all-purpose flour
⅓ cup white wine
1½ cups heavy cream
1 cup milk
¾ teaspoon lemon zest
½ teaspoon ground nutmeg
⅛ teaspoon cayenne pepper
2 cups grated Parmesan cheese
(about 8 ounces)

1. In a 3-quart pot over high heat, bring 2½ quarts water to a boil. Working in 2 batches, blanch kale for 30 seconds. Transfer each batch to a colander and let drain until cool. Squeeze kale to remove excess water, then chop roughly and reserve.
2. Preheat oven to 350°F. Meanwhile, in a large skillet over medium heat, cook onions, butter, ½ teaspoon salt, and freshly ground pepper, stirring frequently, until onions are soft and caramelized, about 25 minutes. Add flour and stir. Add wine and bring to a simmer. Add cream, milk, zest, nutmeg, and cayenne, and simmer for 2 more minutes. Add 1½ cups cheese, reserved kale, and remaining salt, and stir to combine.
3. Pour kale mixture into a 2½-quart baking dish and sprinkle on remaining cheese. Bake until bubbling and brown, 45 to 50 minutes. Serve immediately.

Creamed Kale Gratin

SUMPTUOUS STARTERS & SIDES

Let your meal begin with a salad or soup that sets the stage for the celebratory feast to come. And complement your entrée with special side dishes that go way beyond everyday fare.

Simmered in a full-bodied blend of red wine and cinnamon, the mellow Concorde pear balances bitter greens and tangy blue cheese.

This crisp citrusy salad pairs well with rack of lamb, p. 244, and Onion Pie, p. 238.

FRISÉE SALAD WITH SHIRAZ POACHED PEARS, ROQUEFORT, AND HAZELNUTS

Makes 6 servings *Working time* 20 min.
Total time 45 min., plus cooling

3   Concorde or Bosc pears, peeled, halved, and cored
3   cups Shiraz wine
¾   cup sugar
    Zest and juice of 1½ navel oranges (zest cut into strips, juice strained)
1   cinnamon stick
1   bay leaf
¾   teaspoon vanilla extract
¾   teaspoon fennel seeds
1½ ounces whole hazelnuts (about ⅓ cup)
4½ tablespoons balsamic vinegar
6   tablespoons extra-virgin olive oil
    Salt and freshly ground pepper
2   medium heads frisée, torn into bite-size pieces
3   ounces Roquefort, crumbled

1. Preheat oven to 350°F. Meanwhile, in a medium nonreactive pot over medium-high heat, combine first 8 ingredients (through fennel seeds). Bring liquid to a boil, then reduce to simmer until pears are easily pierced with a paring knife, 25 to 30 minutes. Set aside to cool, about 45 minutes. (At this point, pears can be refrigerated for up to 2 weeks.)
2. Meanwhile, toast hazelnuts on a baking pan until golden, about 10 minutes, tossing occasionally. Transfer hazelnuts to a clean dish towel and rub skins off, then transfer to a cutting board and roughly chop. Set aside.

3. To make dressing: Strain ¾ cup poaching liquid into a small saucepan and cook over medium-high heat until reduced by half, about 10 minutes. Transfer to a medium bowl and stir in vinegar. Whisk in olive oil until combined. Season with salt and pepper.
4. Divide frisée among salad plates. Drizzle with dressing. Sprinkle with Roquefort and reserved hazelnuts. Top each salad with a reserved pear half, cut-side up. Serve with more dressing on the side.

FENNEL, ORANGE, AND OLIVE SALAD

Makes 6 servings *Working time* 20 min.
Total time 20 min.

2   large fennel bulbs, trimmed, cored, and thinly sliced; fronds reserved and chopped
¼   cup fresh orange juice
2   tablespoons fresh lemon juice
1   tablespoon each chopped fresh parsley and chives
½   cup extra-virgin olive oil
    Salt and freshly ground pepper
4   oranges (preferably Valencia), segmented
⅔   cup pitted olives

1. In a small bowl, whisk juices, herbs, and fennel fronds. Slowly add oil until dressing thickens. Season with salt and pepper.
2. In a large bowl, combine sliced fennel bulbs, oranges, and olives. Gently toss with ½ cup dressing. Let marinate for 10 minutes. Divide salad into 6 portions and drizzle each with 2 teaspoons of remaining dressing.

CELERY ROOT SOUP WITH TRUFFLED CROUTONS

Makes 4 servings *Working time* 20 min.
Total time 45 min.

3 tablespoons olive oil, plus more for garnish

3 slices sourdough bread, crusts removed, cut into ½-inch cubes

1 tablespoon chopped fresh parsley

1 tablespoon truffle oil, plus more for garnish

1 medium onion, chopped

2 garlic cloves, chopped

1 large celery root (about 2 pounds), peeled and cut into 1-inch cubes

4 cups vegetable broth

½ cup heavy cream

1 teaspoon salt

½ teaspoon freshly ground pepper

1. In a large pan over medium-high heat, heat 2 tablespoons olive oil. Add bread cubes and sauté until crisp and golden on all sides, about 6 minutes. Transfer to a medium bowl and toss with parsley and truffle oil.

2. In a medium pot over medium heat, heat remaining olive oil. Add onion and garlic and cook until soft, about 5 minutes. Add celery root and vegetable broth; increase heat to high, and bring to a boil. Reduce heat to low and cook until celery root is tender, 15 to 20 minutes.

3. Using an immersion blender, puree soup until smooth. Stir in cream and season with salt and pepper.

4. Divide soup among 4 bowls and garnish with reserved croutons and additional truffle oil. Season with additional salt and pepper, if desired.

BROCCOLI FLORENTINE BISQUE

Makes 6 servings *Working time* 15 min.
Total time 30 min.

1 (5-ounce) package baby spinach

4 tablespoons butter

½ medium sweet onion, diced

5 tablespoons all-purpose flour

4 cups low-sodium chicken stock

4 cups packed fresh broccoli florets

½ cup heavy cream
   Greek yogurt
   Lemon zest

1. Snip end of spinach bag and microwave 2 minutes or until wilted. Squeeze excess liquid from spinach.

2. Sauté onion in melted butter in a large saucepan over medium heat until translucent, about 5 minutes. Add flour and cook, stirring constantly, 1 minute. Whisk in stock; stir in broccoli. Bring to a boil; reduce to a simmer and cook, stirring occasionally, 10 minutes or until broccoli is tender.

3. Stir in wilted spinach and cream. Process soup with an immersion blender (or carefully in batches in a blender) until smooth. Season to taste with salt and pepper. Serve with Greek yogurt and lemon zest.

The irresistible croutons start with sourdough bread.

This gorgeous bright green soup is made of both broccoli and spinach for a super healthy holiday!

Simmered in chicken stock, red creamer potatoes lend velvety texture to Roasted Garlic and Potato Soup with Homemade Croutons.

Fennel, a root vegetable, reminiscent of licorice, is just right for the holidays cooked with nutmeg and Parmesan.

ROASTED GARLIC AND POTATO SOUP WITH HOMEMADE CROUTONS

Makes 6 servings **Working time** 20 min.
Total time 1 hr. 10 min.

1	large head garlic, unpeeled
6	tablespoons extra-virgin olive oil
2	bay leaves
¼	loaf day-old French baguette, cubed
¾	teaspoon sea salt, plus more to taste
1	medium yellow onion, chopped
1	small carrot, chopped
1½	pounds red creamer potatoes, peeled and cut into ½-inch cubes
½	teaspoon freshly ground white pepper, plus more to taste
3	cups low-sodium chicken or vegetable broth
4	ounces Fontina, cut into ¼-inch cubes

1. Preheat oven to 400°F. Using a serrated knife, slice off top ¼ of garlic head, revealing cloves. Place on a 12- by 8-inch sheet of heavy-duty aluminum foil, cut-side up, and drizzle with 1 tablespoon olive oil. Add 1 bay leaf. Fold foil over garlic and seal edges. Roast in a baking dish until garlic cloves are soft and golden brown, about 45 minutes. Transfer to a wire rack and let cool.

2. Meanwhile, on a rimmed baking sheet, toss together bread, 2 tablespoons olive oil, and salt to taste. Bake, stirring once or twice, until golden brown, about 15 minutes. Using a slotted spoon, transfer to a paper-towel-lined plate to drain.

3. In a medium heavy-duty pot over medium-high heat, heat remaining 3 tablespoons olive oil. Add onion, carrot, and potatoes and cook, stirring occasionally, until onion and carrot have softened, 8 to 10 minutes. Mix in ¾ teaspoon salt and ½ teaspoon white pepper and add remaining bay leaf. Add broth and 2 cups water to vegetables, increase heat to high, and bring to a boil. Reduce heat to medium-low and allow soup to simmer until potatoes are very tender, 30 minutes. Remove bay leaf.

4. Squeeze garlic head, from bottom up, to push out each clove into soup; stir. Simmer soup for 5 more minutes, then remove from heat. Using a blender, puree soup. Whisk Fontina into soup over low heat until cheese melts and is fully incorporated. Sprinkle soup with croutons and serve hot.

FENNEL GRATIN

Makes 4 servings **Working time** 15 min.
Total time 50 min.

2	large fennel bulbs, trimmed and halved lengthwise
2	cups whole milk
1	garlic clove
1	bay leaf
	Salt and freshly ground pepper
2½	tablespoons unsalted butter, softened
2½	tablespoons grated Parmigiano-Reggiano
⅛	teaspoon ground nutmeg

1. In a medium pot, arrange fennel in a single layer. Add milk, garlic, bay leaf, and salt and pepper to taste. Partially cover pot and poach fennel over medium-low heat, turning occasionally, until tender, about 45 minutes.

2. Preheat broiler. Coat a medium gratin dish with 1 tablespoon butter. Arrange fennel in dish, cut-side up. Sprinkle with cheese, nutmeg, and pepper to taste. Dot with butter. Broil until golden brown, 1 to 2 minutes.

THE ULTIMATE MASHED POTATOES

Makes 6 servings **Working time** 10 min.
Total time 40 min.

2½ pounds russet potatoes, peeled and
    cut into 2½-inch cubes
    Kosher salt and freshly ground
    pepper
4   tablespoons unsalted butter, melted
¾   cup half-and-half, heated

1. In a large pot, cover potatoes with salted water by 2 inches. Bring to a boil over medium-high heat. Then reduce heat to medium and simmer until potatoes are tender when pierced with a knife, about 25 minutes.

2. Drain potatoes thoroughly in a colander and return to the pot. Add melted butter and, using a potato masher, mash potatoes to desired consistency. (For a smoother texture, pass potatoes through a ricer instead.)

3. Stir in half-and-half and 1 teaspoon salt to combine and until potatoes are creamy. Do not overstir or potatoes will become gluey. Season with additional salt and pepper to taste and serve hot. To punch up this classic dish with savory add-ins, see p. 237.

BRIGHT IDEA! For the fluffiest mash, use super-starchy spuds like russets and skip the food processor—an old-fashioned masher or ricer still works best.

Russets, kosher salt, half-and-half, and a generous dollop (or two) of butter are all it takes to whip up impossibly good holiday-worthy spuds. Want to add more excitement? Check out the yummy add-ins on the next page.

1. Fried Shallots and Crème Fraîche

5. Sauteed Shiitake Mushrooms, Sherry, Dry Mustard, Heavy Cream, and Marjoram

2. Prosciutto, Parmesan, and Parsley

3. Horseradish, Sour Cream, and Freshly Ground Pepper

4. Roquefort, Toasted Walnuts, and Sage

FIVE SCRUMPTUOUS MASHED-POTATO VARIATIONS

Whip up the **Ultimate Mashed Potatoes** on page 234, then stir in one of these mouthwatering flavor combinations.

1. Fried Shallots and Crème Fraîche In a medium skillet over medium-high heat, heat 4 tablespoons oil. Fry 3 large, sliced shallots, until browned and golden, 6 to 8 minutes. (Discard any shallots that over-brown.) Using a slotted spoon, transfer shallots to a paper-towel-lined plate and sprinkle with ¼ teaspoon sea salt. Stir shallots and ⅓ cup crème fraîche into the mashed potatoes.

2. Prosciutto, Parmesan, and Parsley Stir 3 ounces prosciutto, cooked and chopped; 6 tablespoons grated Parmigiano-Reggiano; and 3 tablespoons finely chopped parsley into the mashed potatoes.

3. Horseradish, Sour Cream, and Freshly Ground Pepper Stir ½ cup finely grated fresh horseradish, ½ cup sour cream, and freshly ground pepper to taste into the mashed potatoes.

4. Roquefort, Toasted Walnuts, and Sage Stir 4 ounces Roquefort cheese, crumbled; ⅓ cup chopped walnuts, toasted; and 2 teaspoons chopped fresh sage into the mashed potatoes.

5. Sautéed Shiitake Mushrooms, Sherry, Dry Mustard, Heavy Cream, and Marjoram In a medium skillet over medium-high heat, melt 4 tablespoons unsalted butter. Sauté ½ pound fresh shiitake mushrooms, stemmed and sliced, until tender, about 6 minutes. Add 2 tablespoons sweet sherry and cook until liquid evaporates, about 1 minute. Reduce heat to low and stir in ¼ cup heavy cream, 1 teaspoon dry mustard, and 2 teaspoons chopped fresh marjoram leaves. Cook until cream begins to bubble, 1 to 2 minutes more. Stir mushroom-cream mixture into the mashed potatoes.

ONION PIE

Makes 8 servings *Working time* 20 min.
Total time 1 hr. 50 min.

- 2 tablespoons all-purpose flour, plus more for surface
- 1 (9-inch) piecrust
- 4 tablespoons vegetable oil
- 12 medium onions, thinly sliced
- 1 (16-ounce) container sour cream
- 4 eggs, lightly beaten
- 4 slices bacon, cooked, drained, and chopped
- ½ teaspoon salt
- ½ teaspoon caraway seeds

1. Preheat oven to 425°F. On a lightly floured surface, roll out the piecrust, then arrange in a 9-inch pie pan. Cover with plastic wrap and keep chilled in refrigerator until ready to use.
2. In a large skillet over high heat, heat 2 tablespoons oil. Cook onions, in 2 batches, until browned, about 10 minutes per batch and adding remaining 2 tablespoons oil for second batch.
3. Transfer onions to a large mixing bowl and let cool. Stir in sour cream, eggs, bacon, flour, and salt until well combined. Transfer mixture into piecrust and sprinkle with caraway seeds. Bake until pie is set and top is golden, 50 to 60 minutes. Let sit for 20 minutes before cutting into wedges.

FRENCH GREEN BEANS WITH BUTTER SAUCE AND CRISPY LEEKS

Makes 6 side-dish servings *Working time* 35 min. *Total time* 35 min.

- Vegetable oil, for frying
- ½ cup all-purpose flour
- ½ teaspoon salt
- ½ teaspoon freshly ground pepper
- ½ cup buttermilk
- 2 small leeks (white and light-green parts only), sliced into ⅓-inch thick rounds; plus 2 tablespoons chopped leeks, cleaned well and patted dry
- ½ cup white wine
- 3 tablespoons vinegar
- 2 tablespoons chopped celery
- 1 teaspoon sugar
- 10 tablespoons unsalted butter, cold
- 1½ pounds haricots verts, steamed and kept warm

1. For fried leeks, heat 1 inch oil to 350°F in a heavy pot. Meanwhile, in a bowl, stir flour with ¼ teaspoon each salt and pepper. In another bowl, pour buttermilk. Working in about 4 batches, coat leek rounds in buttermilk, then dredge in flour. Shake off excess flour and fry leeks until golden, about 1 minute. Transfer to paper towels. Repeat with remaining leek rounds.
2. For butter sauce, place white wine, vinegar, celery, chopped leeks, remaining ¼ teaspoon each salt and pepper, and sugar in a pot over medium-high heat. Bring to a boil and cook until liquid is reduced by two-thirds. Whisk in butter, a few pieces at a time, adding more only when fully incorporated into sauce.
3. Transfer steamed green beans to platter, drizzle with butter sauce, and top with fried leeks.

Onion Pie
makes a
great party
appetizer.

Fresh ingredients
put a new spin
on green bean
casserole.

BRIGHT IDEA! Lighten up this classic holiday favorite by skipping
the cream soup and drizzling on a delicious white wine—butter sauce instead.

CHEDDAR BISCUITS

Makes 24 biscuits **Working time** 35 min.
Total time 60 min.

4   cups all-purpose flour, plus more for surface
8   teaspoons baking powder
2   teaspoons salt
2   teaspoons freshly ground pepper
1½ sticks unsalted butter, cold and cut into small pieces
2   cups buttermilk
1   cup grated Cheddar (about 4 ounces)

1. Preheat oven to 450°F. Meanwhile, in a large bowl, combine flour, baking powder, salt, and pepper. Using a pastry cutter or your fingers, cut in butter until mixture resembles coarse crumbs. Add buttermilk and Cheddar, and stir until dough just comes together.
2. Turn out dough onto a lightly floured surface; divide dough into halves and pat each into a rectangle. Set aside one rectangle and cover with a clean dish towel.
3. Working with the other rectangle and using your hands, fold, flatten, and repeat until the dough has been folded over 4 times. Pat out until 1 inch thick. Cut out biscuits using a 2-inch round cutter. Repeat with reserved dough rectangle. Reroll scrap dough and repeat until all dough is used.
4. Transfer biscuits to 2 baking sheets and bake until golden on top, 14 to 18 minutes.

HONEY DINNER ROLLS

Makes 16 rolls **Working time** 30 min.
Total time 1 hr. 10 min., plus rising

⅓   cup plus 1 tablespoon honey, plus more for serving
1   packet active dry yeast
4½ cups all-purpose flour, plus more for surface
¼   cup dry buttermilk powder
1½ teaspoons coarse salt
¼   cup milk
2   large eggs
3   tablespoons unsalted butter, melted, plus more for buttering dishes and serving

1. In a small bowl, combine ½ cup warm water (110°F), ⅓ cup honey, and yeast. Stir to dissolve yeast. Set aside until mixture becomes frothy on top, about 5 minutes.
2. In a large bowl, combine 4 cups flour, buttermilk powder, and salt. Stir in yeast mixture. In a small bowl, whisk together milk, eggs, and 2 tablespoons melted butter. Stir egg mixture into flour mixture and combine until dough comes together. (Add ½ cup flour if dough is too sticky.)
3. Knead dough on a lightly floured surface until smooth, 5 to 8 minutes. Place dough in a buttered bowl. Cover bowl with plastic wrap and let dough rise, at room temperature, until doubled in size, about 45 minutes.

Buy yourself some fridge space by sending guests home with leftovers in dressed-up takeout boxes that look—yep—good enough to eat.

These cheesy biscuits are particularly delicious with our Cola-Glazed Ham (p. 247)!

Honey's said to ensure sweetness for the coming year, a belief that dates at least to Roman times.

The secret to the hearty texture of these rolls is dry buttermilk powder—in a pinch, substitute nondairy coffee creamer.

ELEGANT ENTRÉES

A sprig of rosemary decorating the platter makes this lovely dish even more festive.

HOLIDAY MENU

Ruby Red Grapefruit and Chicory Salad, p. 222

~

Apricot-Stuffed Pork Loin, below

~

Potato and Celery Root Gratin with Gouda, p. 225

~

Creamed Kale Gratin, p. 226

~

Cracked Pepper Dinner Rolls, p. 222

APRICOT-STUFFED PORK LOIN

Makes 10 servings *Working time* 30 min.
Total time 2 hr. 35 min.

11   ounces dried apricots, quartered
1   (4-pound) pork loin
6   garlic cloves, minced
2½   tablespoons fresh rosemary, chopped,
      plus additional sprigs for garnish
1½   cups low-sodium, fat-free chicken
      broth

1. In a medium saucepan over medium-high heat, bring apricots and ½ cup water to a boil. Remove from heat and let sit until water is absorbed, about 10 minutes.

2. Using a long thin knife, cut a 1½-inch-wide slit through center of pork loin lengthwise. Insert a wooden spoon handle and widen the opening. In a small bowl, mix apricots, half the garlic, and ¼ teaspoon salt. Pack mixture into opening in pork loin.

3. Tie pork loin at 1½-inch intervals with 10 to 12-inch lengths of kitchen twine.

4. Preheat oven to 325°F. Using a mortar and pestle, grind together chopped rosemary, ¾ teaspoon salt, and 1 teaspoon pepper to a coarse rub. Mix in remaining garlic and rub all over pork loin.

5. Place pork loin in a medium roasting pan fitted with a rack and roast for 45 minutes. Remove from oven and pour broth over pork loin. Return to oven and continue to roast, basting every 15 minutes, until the meat's internal temperature reaches 150°F, up to 1 more hour.

6. Transfer roast to a wire rack to rest for 20 minutes before slicing. Garnish with rosemary sprigs. Meanwhile, strain pan juices into a gravy boat (reheat in a small saucepan over low heat if necessary).

HOLIDAY MENU

Broccoli Florentine Bisque, p. 230

~

Fennel, Orange, and Olive Salad, p. 229

~

Cherry-and-Port-Glazed Rack of Lamb, below

~

Onion Pie, p. 238

~

Honey Dinner Rolls, p. 240

CHERRY-AND-PORT-GLAZED RACK OF LAMB

Makes 8 servings **Working time** *15 min.*
Total time *About 50 min.*

1½ cups cherry preserves
¾   cup ruby port
1   garlic clove, smashed
4   fresh thyme sprigs, plus 1 tablespoon
    chopped thyme leaves
¾   teaspoon sea salt
1   teaspoon freshly ground pepper
2   lamb racks (8 ribs per rack, about
    2 pounds each), excess fat trimmed
    and bones frenched

1. Preheat oven to 450°F. Line a roasting pan with aluminum foil and set aside. In a small saucepan over medium heat, bring cherry preserves, port, garlic, and thyme sprigs to a boil. Let boil for 2 to 3 minutes, then remove from heat. Reserve ⅓ of sauce for basting and set aside remaining for serving.

2. In a small bowl, combine chopped thyme, sea salt, and pepper and rub over lamb. Set racks upright in prepared pan by propping them against each other, with meaty sides facing out and bones criss-crossing. Roast lamb for 15 minutes. Continue to roast lamb, basting with reserved cherry-port sauce every 5 minutes, until meat reaches desired doneness—an additional 10 minutes for rare, 15 for medium-rare, 20 for medium. Allow lamb to rest for 15 to 20 minutes. Carve between ribs and serve with reserved sauce.

HOLIDAY MENU

Marvin Woods's Brussels Sprouts, Red Pepper, and Avocado Salad, p. 225

~

Sweet and Spicy Cola-Glazed Ham, below

~

French Green Beans with Butter Sauce and Crispy Leeks, p. 238

~

Mashed Potatoes with Roquefort, Toasted Walnuts, and Sage, p. 237

~

Cheddar Biscuits, p. 240

SWEET AND SPICY COLA-GLAZED HAM

Makes 12 servings **Working time** 15 min.
Total time 3 hr. 35 min.

16 ounces cola (2 cups)
1   cup dark-brown sugar
½   cup Dijon mustard
1   tablespoon red pepper flakes
1   (6- to 8-pound) bone-in cooked ham
    Butter, for aluminum foil

1. In a medium saucepan over medium-high heat, bring cola, brown sugar, mustard, and red pepper flakes to a boil. Reduce heat to low, and simmer until glaze is reduced and slightly thickened, 20 to 30 minutes.

2. Preheat oven to 350°F. Meanwhile, using a sharp knife, score ham, making ½-inch deep marks in a grid pattern. Line a roasting pan with a piece of buttered aluminum foil. Transfer ham to pan and, using a pastry brush, cover with ⅓ of the glaze.

3. Bake ham for 1½ hours, and brush with ⅓ of the glaze. Bake for another hour, and brush with remaining glaze. Continue baking for up to 30 minutes more, until an instant-read thermometer reaches 145°F when inserted into ham. Remove from oven and let rest for 20 minutes. Serve with Cheddar Biscuits (see p. 240 for recipe) and store-bought chutneys and mustards.

Bourbon-Cranberry
Bread Pudding (p. 251)
is a satisfying ending to
a holiday dinner.

Sweet! Cakes, Pies, Cookies, and More

Every family has its favorite recipes for holiday treats—but there's always room for something new. Feast your eyes on this treasury of Christmas desserts—both classics, and updated twists on treasured tradition.

VANILLA YOGURT & BERRY TRIFLE

Makes 10 servings **Working time** 20 min.
Total time 35 min., plus chilling

2   packages (10 ounces each) frozen strawberries, thawed, strained, and juice reserved
1   package (12-ounce) frozen raspberries, thawed, strained, and juice reserved
1⅓ cups confectioners' sugar
1½ teaspoons cornstarch
¾   cup heavy cream
3   containers (16 ounces each) nonfat vanilla Greek yogurt, such as Chobani
40 ladyfingers
2   tablespoons orange liqueur (optional), such as Cointreau
1   package (16-ounce) frozen blueberries, thawed and drained

1. In a medium saucepan over medium heat, whisk together raspberry and strawberry juices with ⅔ cup sugar and cornstarch. Boil until thickened, 1 to 2 minutes. Transfer to a medium bowl and refrigerate until cool, about 20 minutes.
2. Meanwhile, in a medium bowl, whip heavy cream to stiff peaks; set aside. In a large bowl, combine yogurt and remaining ⅔ cup sugar. Fold in whipped cream.
3. Break ladyfingers in half. Place half of them in a 2-quart glass bowl or trifle dish. Drizzle cookies with 1 tablespoon liqueur, if using, and dollop with ⅓ of yogurt mixture. Spoon half of berries over yogurt mixture, then drizzle 3 to 4 tablespoons thickened juices. Layer another ⅓ of yogurt mixture over berries, followed by a layer of remaining ladyfingers. Drizzle with remaining 1 tablespoon liqueur and dollop with remaining yogurt mixture. Top with remaining berries and 3 to 4 more tablespoons thickened juice. Refrigerate until chilled, about 2 hours, before serving.

BOURBON-CRANBERRY BREAD PUDDING

Makes 8 servings **Working time** 1 hr.
Total time 1 hr. 50 min.

2½ tablespoons unsalted butter, plus more for pan
9   large eggs
1   egg yolk
1⅔ cups granulated sugar
3½ cups whole milk
⅔   cups heavy cream
6   teaspoons vanilla extract
2¾ teaspoons ground cinnamon
¼   teaspoons freshly grated nutmeg
10 slices country white bread, toasted and cut into 1-inch squares
4½ cups fresh or frozen cranberries
¼   cup pecans, toasted
½   cup maple syrup
1   tablespoon bourbon
    Confectioners' sugar, for sprinkling

1. Preheat oven to 350°F. Butter an 8½- by 4½-inch loaf pan. Cut a piece of parchment to a length of 26 inches. Fold in thirds lengthwise so that it becomes 4½ inches wide. Lightly butter the paper and fit it inside the pan along all four sides, buttered side facing in; make sure at least 1½ inches extend beyond the top of the pan rim. Place loaf pan on a baking pan and set aside.
2. In a medium bowl and using an electric beater, beat 2 eggs and 1 yolk with ⅔ cup granulated sugar until very thick and pale. In a large pan over medium heat, combine 2 cups milk, heavy cream, 1½ tablespoons butter, 4 teaspoons vanilla, 1¼ teaspoons cinnamon, and nutmeg. Cook, stirring occasionally, just until bubbles form around edge of pan. Remove from heat.

Gradually stir milk-cream mixture, a tablespoon at a time, into beaten eggs. Then, gradually return entire mixture to the pan.
3. Add bread, ½ cup cranberries, and pecans to milk-cream-egg mixture and gently stir to mix, making sure all bread is soaked. Transfer to prepared loaf pan and bake until set and a knife inserted into center comes out clean, about 45 minutes. Transfer pan to a wire rack to cool. Remove from pan to cool completely. Cover with plastic wrap and refrigerate until ready to serve, or up to 1 day.
4. Meanwhile, in a medium bowl and using an electric beater, beat together 4 eggs, maple syrup, bourbon, and remaining vanilla. In a medium saucepan over medium heat, warm remaining milk just until bubbles form around edge of pan; cool slightly. Add bourbon mixture. Cook over low heat, stirring constantly, until thickened, about 5 minutes (do not allow mixture to boil). Strain into a bowl and stir to cool slightly. Cover with plastic wrap and refrigerate until ready to serve, or up to 1 day.
5. In a medium pan, bring ¾ cup water and remaining cranberries and sugar to a boil, stirring occasionally. Cook until berries just begin to pop. Let cool, then cover with plastic wrap and refrigerate until ready to serve, or up to 1 day.
6. Cut reserved bread pudding into 8 slices. Stir remaining eggs and cinnamon together in a pie plate. In a large skillet over medium heat, melt 1 tablespoon butter. Working with 1 slice at a time, dip bread pudding into egg mixture. Cook, about 3 to 4 minutes per side. Repeat with remaining slices. To serve, spoon reserved bourbon custard on a platter. Place bread pudding slice on custard and top with reserved cranberry sauce. Sprinkle with confectioners' sugar.

This delectable skillet crumble gets its old-fashioned goodness from brown sugar and cinnamon.

BERRY CRUMBLE

Makes 10 servings *Working time* 10 min. *Total time* 45 min.

- 3 cups oats
- ½ cup all-purpose flour, plus 2 tablespoons
- 1 cup chopped pecans
- 1 cup dark-brown sugar
- 1 cup granulated sugar, divided
- 2 teaspoons cinnamon
  Zest of 2 oranges, divided
- 2 sticks unsalted butter, cut into small pieces
- 5 cups frozen raspberries and/or blackberries
- 2 cups frozen blueberries

1. Preheat oven to 400°F. In a large bowl, toss together oats, ½ cup flour, pecans, brown sugar, ½ cup granulated sugar, cinnamon, and zest of 1 orange. Add butter and gently press with fingers to incorporate into mixture; set aside. **2.** Place berries in a 12-inch skillet. Sprinkle with remaining ½ cup granulated sugar, zest of 1 orange, and 2 tablespoons flour and gently toss. Scatter oat mixture over berries. Transfer to oven and bake until fruit is bubbly and topping is golden, about 35 minutes.

MAPLE GRANOLA PECAN PIE

Makes 8 servings **Working time** 35 *min.* **Total time** 2 hrs. 35 min.

1 cup regular oats
⅛ teaspoon ground cinnamon
6 tablespoons melted butter, divided
1 cup grade B maple syrup, plus 2 tablespoons for oats
1½ cups pecan halves and pieces
½ cups sweetened flaked coconut
½ package (14.1-ounce) refrigerated piecrusts
½ cup firmly packed brown sugar
2 teaspoons all-purpose flour
¼ teaspoon salt
3 large eggs
2 teaspoons vanilla extract

1. Heat oven to 350°F. In a small bowl, stir together oats, cinnamon, 2 tablespoons melted butter, and 2 tablespoons maple syrup until blended. Spread oat mixture on a lightly greased baking sheet. Bake 20 minutes or until oats begin to turn golden; remove from oven and stir in pecans and coconut. Bake 10 to 12 more minutes or until pecans and coconut are lightly toasted. Remove from oven and cool completely on a wire rack (about 15 minutes).

2. Fit refrigerated piecrust into a 9-inch pieplate according to package directions; fold edges under and crimp as desired.

3. Whisk together brown sugar and next 2 ingredients until blended.

Add eggs, vanilla, remaining 4 tablespoons melted butter, and remaining 1 cup maple syrup, whisking until blended. Spoon pecan mixture into prepared piecrust; carefully pour maple syrup mixture over pecan mixture.

4. Bake at 350°F on lower oven rack for 35 to 40 minutes or until set. Remove from oven and cool completely on a wire rack (about 1 hour).

APPLE CROSTATA

Makes 8 servings **Working time** 45 *min.* **Total time** 1 hr. 55 min.

4 large Granny Smith apples (about 2 pounds)
4 large Golden Delicious apples (about 2 pounds)
½ cup butter
1 cup brown sugar
½ cup red pepper jelly (such as Braswell's)
½ teaspoon ground cinnamon
¾ cup (5 ounces) dried Montmorency cherries
⊠ cup sweetened dried cranberries
1 package (14.1-ounce) refrigerated piecrusts
1 large egg, beaten
1½ tablespoons turbinado sugar
2 tablespoons pepitas

1. Peel apples and cut into ½-inch-thick wedges. In a large skillet, melt butter over medium-high heat; add brown sugar and next 2 ingredients and bring to a boil. Add apples and cook, stirring often, 20 minutes or until apples are tender. Stir in dried cherries and cranberries.

Remove apple mixture from skillet using a slotted spoon, and let cool. Cook remaining liquid in skillet over medium heat 10 minutes or until thickened to a syrup-like consistency.

2. Heat oven to 425°F. Unroll piecrusts, and stack on a lightly floured surface. Roll stacked piecrusts into a 15-inch circle, and place on a parchment-lined baking sheet. Mound apple mixture in center of piecrust leaving a 3-inch border around edges. Lift pastry edges, and pull up over apple mixture leaving a 6-inch circle of fruit showing in center; press folds gently to secure. Brush beaten egg over pastry, and sprinkle with turbinado sugar. Place the lightly greased sides of a 9-inch springform pan with clasp open around tart; close clasp.

3. Bake at 425°F on lower oven rack for 35 to 40 minutes or until golden brown. Run a knife around edges of tart to loosen. Cool on a wire rack 30 minutes; remove pan sides. Sprinkle top of tart with pepitas. Serve with reserved sauce.

Whip up a batch of these irrisistible, individual bite-sized morsels.

BRIGHT IDEA! Dress the cake with fresh whipped cream or a medley of roasted or poached fruit.

Burnt-Sugar Pound Cake is a tender holiday treat.

BURNT-SUGAR POUND CAKE

Makes *One 9- by 5-inch cake*
Working time *40 min.* **Total time** *1 hr. 45 min., including cooling*

2⅔	cups sugar
3	teaspoons lemon juice
2	teaspoons vanilla extract
2	cups flour
½	teaspoon salt
1	cup (2 sticks) unsalted butter, room temperature
1	vanilla bean, split lengthwise and seeds scraped
5	large eggs

1. Make the burnt-sugar syrup: Heat oven to 325°F. Butter and flour one 8-cup (9- by 5- by 3-inch) loaf pan and set aside. Bring a small pot of water to simmer and maintain. Place 1⅓ cups sugar and 1 teaspoon lemon juice in a small, nonstick saucepan over medium heat and cook until the sugar at the edges of the pan begins to bubble. Remove from the heat and stir until liquefied and dark amber—about 2 minutes. Let sit for 1 minute. Slowly add 1 cup of the simmering water. The mixture will steam and thicken. Return to the stovetop over low heat, stirring occasionally until smooth—about 15 minutes. Carefully measure out ¼ cup syrup. Set aside. Add 1 teaspoon vanilla extract and the remaining lemon juice to the remaining syrup and keep warm.
2. Make the batter: Sift the flour and salt together into a medium bowl. Cream the butter, remaining sugar, and the vanilla bean seeds together in a large bowl using an electric mixer set on high speed. Add the eggs, one at a time, blending thoroughly after each addition. Add the reserved ¼ cup burnt-sugar syrup, remaining vanilla extract, and the flour, in fourths, mixing thoroughly with each addition. Pour the batter into the pan and bake until a skewer inserted into the center of the cake comes out clean—about 1 hour. Cool for 5 minutes before unmolding. Brush the warm cake with ½ cup of the burnt-sugar syrup. Serve at room temperature with the remaining syrup.

MINI BROWN-SUGAR CHEESECAKES

Makes *24 cheesecakes*
Working time *20 min.*
Total time *50 min., plus chilling*

1¼	cups (about 1 sleeve of 4-section graham crackers from a 14.4-ounce box) graham cracker crumbs
3	tablespoons granulated sugar
¼	teaspoon salt
5	tablespoons unsalted butter, melted, plus more for pan
2	packages (8 ounces each) cream cheese, softened
2	large eggs
2	tablespoons (about 1 lemon) fresh lemon juice
1	tablespoon (about 1 lemon) lemon zest
1	tablespoon vanilla extract
1	teaspoon ground ginger
1	cup light brown sugar
½	cup thinly sliced candied ginger

1. Preheat oven to 350°F. Meanwhile, in a small bowl, combine graham cracker crumbs, granulated sugar, and salt. Add butter and stir until combined. Spoon about 1 tablespoon mixture into each cup of a buttered 24-cup mini muffin pan; press down to form a solid bottom layer. Bake for about 5 minutes. Transfer pan to a wire rack to cool. Reduce oven to 300°F.
2. In the bowl of a stand mixer, beat cream cheese until light and fluffy, about 2 minutes. With beater running, add eggs, 1 at a time. Add lemon juice and zest, vanilla, ground ginger, and brown sugar and beat until combined. Divide filling equally among muffin cups and bake until firm, 15 to 20 minutes. Transfer to a wire rack and let cool completely. Refrigerate until set, at least 4 hours or overnight.
3. Gently run a knife around the cheesecakes' edges to loosen them, and invert pan to release the cakes. Transfer to a cake stand and garnish with candied ginger.

BRIGHT IDEA! To save time, premeasure a few batches of the dry ingredients and seal them in airtight bags so you'll have "cake mix" at the ready for last-minute desserts.

DEEP DARK CHOCOLATE CAKE

Makes *Two 8-inch round layers (10 servings)*
Working time *40 min.* **Total time** *1 hr. 35 min.*

2	cups all-purpose flour
1	cup cocoa
2	cups granulated sugar
1	teaspoon baking soda
1	teaspoon baking powder
1	teaspoon salt
2	large eggs
1	teaspoon pure vanilla extract
1	cup sour cream
½	cup canola oil
1	teaspoon white vinegar
1	cup unsalted butter, softened
¾	cup raspberry jam, strained and seeds discarded
1½	cups confectioners' sugar

1. Heat oven to 350°F. Butter two 8-inch-round cake pans and line bottoms with parchment. Combine flour, cocoa, granulated sugar, baking soda, baking powder, and salt together in a large bowl. Add eggs, vanilla, sour cream, oil, vinegar (for leavening and a more tender cake), and 1 cup hot water and mix with a wooden spoon until batter is smooth.

2. Pour batter into prepared pans and bake until a wooden skewer, inserted into cake center, comes out clean, 35 to 40 minutes. Cool cakes in pans 20 minutes; release from pans and cool completely on wire racks.

3. Beat butter and jam together using an electric mixer set on medium speed until fluffy. Add confectioners' sugar and beat until smooth. Spread filling between 2 cake layers and frost with Superquick Chocolate Buttercream (see below).

Superquick Chocolate Buttercream

Using a mixer set on medium-high speed, beat **1 cup butter** (2 sticks) and **6 ounces melted and slightly cooled bittersweet chocolate** together until fluffy. Reduce speed to medium and beat in **2 cups marshmallow cream**. Add **¼ teaspoon vanilla extract** and **6 tablespoons confectioners' sugar** and increase speed to medium-high and beat, scraping down the sides of the bowl occasionally, until smooth and fluffy. Chill for 20 minutes before using. **Makes** *4 cups.*

This impressive-looking Molten Chocolate Cake is both light and rich.

Healthy holidays: Swapping in apple sauce for butter and using nonfat cream cheese saves 215 calories and 19 grams of fat per slice.

MOLTEN CHOCOLATE CAKE

Makes 4 cakes *Working time* 15 min. *Total time* 30 min.

1½	sticks unsalted butter, plus more for buttering ramekins
6	ounces bittersweet chocolate, chopped
3	tablespoons cocoa powder
3	large eggs
3	large egg yolks
⅓	cup granulated sugar, plus 2 tablespoons
¼	cup all-purpose flour
2	tablespoons confectioners' sugar, for dusting

1. Preheat oven to 450°F. In a heatproof bowl set over simmering water, or in the top of a double boiler, melt butter and chocolate. Meanwhile, butter four 6-ounce ramekins and coat all with 2 tablespoons cocoa powder; tap out excess. Transfer ramekins to a baking sheet and set aside. Remove chocolate mixture from heat and set aside to let cool slightly.

2. In a medium bowl, whisk together eggs, yolks, and granulated sugar. Stir in reserved chocolate mixture, then stir in flour and remaining cocoa powder until just combined. Divide batter among ramekins and bake until cakes are firm yet soft in center, 13 to 14 minutes. Transfer to a wire rack and let cool slightly, about 1 minute.

3. Invert ramekins onto serving plates to release cakes. Dust tops with confectioners' sugar.

CHOCOLATE CAKE WITH CHOCOLATE-ORANGE SAUCE

Makes 12 servings *Working time* 20 min. *Total time* 1 hr. 20 min., plus cooking

	Butter, for greasing pan and parchment
1¾	cups all-purpose flour
1⅔	cups granulated sugar
1	cup unsweetened cocoa, plus 2 teaspoons
2½	teaspoons baking soda
½	teaspoon salt
3	large egg whites
1	cup low-fat buttermilk
⅔	cup applesauce
2	tablespoons canola oil
4	ounces nonfat cream cheese, softened
1¼	cups confectioners' sugar
½	cup orange juice
2	teaspoons orange liqueur (optional)

1. Preheat oven to 350°F. Butter a nonstick 9-inch cake pan. Cut and butter a circle of parchment to fit into bottom of pan. Set pan aside.

2. In a large bowl, sift flour, sugar, ½ cup cocoa, baking soda, and salt; set aside. In a medium bowl, beat egg whites until glossy and soft peaks form. Using a rubber spatula, stir buttermilk, applesauce, and oil into flour mixture until combined and batter is smooth. Fold egg whites into batter and transfer to prepared pan.

3. Bake cake, with rack set in the middle, until a toothpick inserted into center tests clean, 40 to 45 minutes. Transfer pan to a wire rack and let cool for 20 minutes. Invert cake and let cool completely.

4. Meanwhile, in a medium bowl, beat together cream cheese, confectioners' sugar, and ½ cup cocoa. In a medium pot over medium-high heat, bring juice to a boil and cook until reduced by half, 2 to 3 minutes. Add juice to cocoa mixture and stir until combined and the consistency of molasses. Pass sauce through a fine strainer for a smooth and silky consistency. Stir in orange liqueur, if desired. Sift remaining 2 teaspoons cocoa over cake. Slice cake, spoon sauce over each slice, and serve.

TURTLE-CANDY TART

Makes 16 slices *Working time* 35 min.
Total time 1 hr. 35 min., plus chilling

2	sticks unsalted butter
14	(about 1½ cups) chocolate graham crackers, crushed
⅓	cup granulated sugar
	Sea salt
1	cup light-brown sugar
1	cup sweetened condensed milk
½	cup light corn syrup
6	ounces (about 1½ cups) pecan halves, toasted
¾	teaspoon vanilla
8	ounces bittersweet chocolate, finely chopped
2½	cups heavy cream

1. Preheat oven to 375°F. Meanwhile, in a small pot over medium-low heat, melt 1 stick butter. Transfer to a medium bowl. Add graham crackers, granulated sugar, and ½ teaspoon sea salt and combine. Press mixture into the bottom and along the sides of an 11-inch tart pan with a removable bottom. Bake crust for 10 minutes. Transfer pan to a wire rack and cool, about 20 minutes.

2. Meanwhile, make the caramel: In a medium pot fitted with a candy thermometer, melt remaining butter over medium heat. Add brown sugar, condensed milk, corn syrup, and ½ teaspoon sea salt and stir to combine. Allow caramel to come to a boil; maintain gentle boil, stirring constantly, until mixture reaches 240°F, about 10 minutes. Stir in pecans and vanilla. Pour caramel into tart crust and spread evenly. Set aside to cool, about 30 minutes.

3. Meanwhile, make the ganache: Place chocolate in a medium bowl. In a small pot, bring 1 cup heavy cream to a boil and pour over chocolate. Let sit for 30 seconds, then stir until melted. Pour over caramel and spread ganache into a smooth, even layer with a spatula. Refrigerate tart until set, about 1 hour.

4. Meanwhile, in a medium bowl and using an electric mixer, beat remaining heavy cream until soft peaks form. Refrigerate until ready to serve. Once tart is set, remove outer ring of pan. Let sit at room temperature for 20 minutes before serving. Serve with dollops of whipped cream.

PRALINE TURTLE CAKE

Makes 16 slices *Working time* 40 min.
Total time 1 hr. 30 min.

½	cup butter
1	cup brown sugar
1	can (14 ounces) sweetened condensed milk
1	cup chopped pecans
2	cups all-purpose flour
¾	cup unsweetened cocoa
2	cups granulated sugar
1½	teaspoons baking powder
1½	teaspoons baking soda
1	teaspoon salt
2	large eggs
1	cup sour cream
½	cup canola oil
1	teaspoon vanilla extract
1	teaspoon white vinegar
½	cup fudge topping
½	cup chocolate chips, melted

1. Make the cake: Heat oven to 350°F. Butter the bottoms of two 9-inch round cake pans and fit a circle of parchment large enough to cover 1 inch up the side of each cake pan. Heat the butter, brown sugar, and sweetened condensed milk in a 2-quart saucepan over medium heat until the butter melts and the sugar is dissolved. Do not boil. Divide the sugar mixture between the prepared pans. Sprinkle ¾ cup pecans over sugar mixture and set aside to cool. Combine the flour, cocoa, granulated sugar, baking powder, baking soda, and salt together in a large bowl. Add the eggs, sour cream, oil, vanilla, and vinegar, and 1 cup hot water and mix with a wooden spoon until the batter is smooth. Pour the batter into the cake pans—over sugar mixture—and bake until a wooden skewer inserted into the cake center comes out clean—35 to 40 minutes. Cool cakes in the pans for 10 minutes. Run a knife around the edge of the pans and turn cakes out onto a cooling rack. Remove the paper and cool completely.

2. Assemble the cake: Spread the fudge topping over the sugar mixture side of 1 cake layer. Place the second layer over the first and drizzle with the melted chocolate chips and the remaining ¼ cup pecans. Frost the cake sides with your favorite chocolate icing.

Brown sugar, pecans, chocolate chips—what's not to like about Praline Turtle Cake?

For the cleanest cut, slice Turtle-Candy Tart while it's still cold.

BRIGHT IDEA!

To split a vanilla bean open, use a small, sharp paring knife and cut from one tip to the other. Carefully separate the two long, flat sides and scrape the seeds into the dish you're preparing. Save the pods for steeping or grinding into powder, or use them to make vanilla sugar.

Treat yourself and those you love with these delicious crêpes.

ROASTED APPLES WITH SALTED MAPLE CREAM

Makes 6 servings *Working time* 15 min. *Total time* 1 hr. 15 min.

4   tablespoons unsalted butter, softened
2   vanilla beans, split, seeds scraped and pods reserved
¼   teaspoon salt
6   tablespoons maple syrup
4   tablespoons Cointreau
½   teaspoon vanilla extract
6   tart, red apples, such as Braeburn or Rome
1   cup heavy cream

1. Heat oven to 450°F. Stir butter, vanilla bean seeds, and ⅛ teaspoon salt together. Set aside. Combine 4 tablespoons maple syrup, the Cointreau, vanilla extract, and ½ cup water. Set aside.
2. Cut off the top ⅓ of each apple and scoop out a small bowl in the apple's center. (Leave ½ inch of flesh in the bottom and 1 inch around the walls.) Place the apples in a large baking dish. Spread each apple cavity with the butter mixture and drizzle with the syrup mixture.
3. Place a piece of vanilla bean pod in each apple and roast for 10 minutes. Tip the apples and generously baste with the spilled liquid. Continue to roast, basting every 10 to 15 minutes, until the apples are soft—45 to 50 minutes. Let cool for 5 minutes.
4. Whisk the cream with the remaining maple syrup and salt until foamy and doubled in volume. Serve immediately over warm apples.

CRÊPES WITH VANILLA POACHED APRICOTS AND MASCARPONE CREAM

Makes 6 crepes *Working time* 35 min. *Total time* 6 hrs.

16   ounces dried apricots (2 cups)
½   cup sugar
½   cup white wine
2   vanilla beans, split and scraped
¾   cup milk
¼   cup milk, warmed to 110°F (see step 2)
1½   teaspoons active dry yeast
1   cup all-purpose flour
3   large eggs
4   tablespoons butter, melted
⅛   teaspoons salt
1½   teaspoons vanilla extract
     Mascarpone Cream (see right)

1. Poach the apricots: Combine the apricots, ¼ cup sugar, white wine, vanilla beans, and ¾ cup water in a high-sided skillet and heat to a boil over medium heat. Reduce heat to low, cover, and simmer until soft—50 to 60 minutes. Uncover and bring to a boil over high heat. Boil for 2 minutes.
2. Make the batter: Stir the warmed milk, yeast, and ⅛ teaspoon sugar together in a medium bowl and let sit until foamy and doubled in size—15 to 20 minutes. Sift the flour through a fine-mesh sieve over the eggs in a large bowl and whisk to combine. Stir in the melted butter and add the remaining sugar, salt, vanilla extract, and the milk mixture. Gently whisk in the remaining milk. Scrape down the sides of the bowl. Let sit until doubled—3 to 4 hours at room

temperature or overnight in the refrigerator.
3. Make the crepes: Lightly brush a nonstick medium skillet with some butter and heat over medium-high heat. Stir the batter with a whisk and pour ¼ cup batter into the skillet. Tilt to distribute. Cook until the underside is golden brown—about 45 seconds. Flip the crêpe and continue to cook for 30 more seconds. Transfer crêpe to a sheet of waxed paper. Repeat with remaining batter; stack crêpes between sheets of waxed paper. Cover with a warm, damp cloth. Fill each of 6 crêpes with ⅓ cup apricots and ¼ cup Mascarpone Cream (see recipe below). Fold and serve immediately. To store remaining crêpes, wrap in plastic wrap and freeze for up to 3 weeks.

Mascarpone Cream

Makes 4 cups *Working time* 5 min. *Total time* 35 min.

1   cup (8 ounces) mascarpone cheese
2   cups heavy cream
¼   cup sugar
1   teaspoon lemon zest

Place all the ingredients in a medium bowl and whip with an electric mixer set on medium-high speed until soft, fluffy peaks form—1 to 2 minutes. Transfer to a clean bowl, cover, and chill for up to 30 minutes.

To create these sweet cookie name tags, follow the recipe for Sugar Cookies (at right). Form the cookies with a tag-shaped cutters, then use a plastic straw to punch a hole in the pointed end of each treat before baking.

SUGAR COOKIES

Makes about 16 cookies *Working time* 35 min. *Total time* 2 hr. 45 min.

1. In a large bowl, using a mixer set on medium-high, beat together **2 sticks softened unsalted butter** and **1 cup sugar** until fluffy. Add **3 large eggs**, one at a time, followed by **1½ teaspoons vanilla extract** and **½ teaspoon salt**. Reduce mixer speed to low and gradually add **3¼ cups all-purpose flour**, beating until ingredients are combined. (Dough will be slightly sticky.) Divide dough into 4 equal portions and cover each in plastic wrap, patting into ½-inch thick squares. Chill until firm, about 2 hours or overnight.

2. Preheat oven to 400°F. On a floured surface, roll out dough, a square at a time, to ½ inch thick. Cut out cookies using ornament- or tag-shaped cutters. Transfer cookies to a parchment-lined baking sheet and chill for 10 minutes. Bake until lightly golden, about 12 minutes. Cool completely on pan or wire rack before decorating.

MAKE THIS EASY ICING IN UNDER A MINUTE!

With an electric mixer on low, beat **⅔ cup confectioners' sugar**, **2 teaspoons meringue powder**, and **2 tablespoons water** until smooth and mixture flows easily. To achieve the vibrant designs shown above, tint the icing with gel food coloring and transfer it to piping bags fitted with small round tips. Refer to the photographs above as a decorating guide, adding colored sugar and dragées to wet icing if desired.

Simple sugar cookies go glamorous, thanks to ornament-shaped cutters and colorful icing.

Fresh, ground, and candied gingers give these cookies real kick.

Mouthwatering oatmeal cookies are a classic!

TRIPLE-GINGER COOKIES

Makes 40 cookies *Working time* 30 min.
Total time 1 hr. 45 min.

2 cups whole-wheat flour
1 tablespoon ground ginger
1 teaspoon baking soda
   Salt
1 stick butter
¼ cup molasses
⅔ cup light brown sugar
2 tablespoons finely grated fresh ginger
1 large egg, beaten
1 cup dried apricots, finely chopped
½ cup finely chopped crystallized ginger
1 cup turbinado sugar

1. In a large bowl, stir together flour, ground ginger, baking soda, and a pinch of salt. Set aside.
2. In a small pan over medium-low heat, melt butter. Remove from heat and stir in molasses, brown sugar, and fresh ginger. Let cool.
3. Add egg to cooled molasses mixture and stir to combine. Slowly stir into reserved dry ingredients, then stir in apricots and crystallized ginger. Cover with plastic wrap and chill for 1 hour.
4. Preheat oven to 350°F. Meanwhile, place turbinado sugar in a shallow bowl. Shape dough into ½-inch balls, then roll in turbinado sugar. Place cookies on 2 parchment-lined baking sheets, leaving 2 inches between cookies. Bake for 8 to 10 minutes. Transfer to a wire rack to cool.

GRANDMA MOLLIE'S OATMEAL RAISIN-CHOCOLATE CHIP COOKIES

Makes 4 dozen cookies *Working time* 30 min.
Total time 45 min.

2 sticks unsalted butter, softened
1 cup sugar
2 eggs, lightly beaten
2 cups all-purpose flour
2 cups old-fashioned oats
1 teaspoon baking powder
1 teaspoon baking soda
¼ teaspoon salt
1 teaspoon cinnamon
1 cup raisins
½ cup coarsely chopped walnuts
1¼ cups chocolate chips
¼ cup milk

1. Preheat oven to 350°F. Line a baking sheet with parchment and set aside.
2. In a medium bowl, cream butter and sugar together until light and fluffy. Stir in eggs until well combined. In a separate bowl, combine all dry ingredients, plus raisins, walnuts, and chocolate chips. Add dry mixture to wet mixture and stir to combine. Stir in milk.
3. Drop dough in heaping tablespoonfuls, about 1 inch apart, on the baking sheet. Bake until golden brown and slightly crunchy, about 15 minutes.

CHOCOLATE CHUNK AND CHERRY COOKIES

Makes 4 dozen cookies *Working time* 25 min.
Total time 40 min.

1½ cups all-purpose flour
1   cup cocoa
1   teaspoon salt
1   teaspoon baking soda
1   cup unsalted butter
¾   cup granulated sugar
1¼   cups (firmly packed) dark brown sugar
2   large eggs
2   teaspoons pure vanilla extract
1½   cups chopped bittersweet chocolate
1½   cups dried tart cherries

1. Heat oven to 350°F. Line baking pans with parchment and set aside. Combine flour, cocoa, salt, and baking soda in a medium bowl and set aside. Beat butter and sugars in a large bowl until light and fluffy, using a mixer set on medium-high speed. Beat in eggs one at a time and add vanilla.
2. Reduce mixer speed to low and gradually add flour mixture until combined. Stir in chopped chocolate and cherries (for blond **Milk Chocolate and Cherry Cookies**, omit cocoa, add an additional cup flour, and replace bittersweet chocolate with milk chocolate). Shape 2 tablespoons dough into rough balls and place 2 inches apart on a baking sheet lined with parchment.
3. Bake 11 to 13 minutes. Cool cookies on pan 2 minutes. Transfer to a wire rack and let cool completely.

PECAN PRALINES

Makes 16 pralines *Working time* 15 min.
Total time 1 hr.

5   tablespoons unsalted butter, plus more for parchment
1   cup light brown sugar
1   cup granulated sugar
1   cup melted vanilla-bean ice cream
9½   ounces pecans, chopped (2½ cups)
½   teaspoon salt

1. Line 2 baking pans with parchment, butter parchment, and set aside. In a medium pot over medium-low heat, combine sugars and ice cream, stirring with a clean, metal spoon until sugars are dissolved. Using a pastry brush dipped in water, brush down sides of pot to prevent sugars from crystallizing.
2. Add 5 tablespoons butter and stir to combine. Fit pot with a candy thermometer, increase heat to medium, and let cook until mixture reaches 240°F. Remove pot from heat and stir in pecans and salt. until slightly opaque, 30 to 60 seconds.
3. Drop praline mixture, by 2 heaping tablespoons, onto prepared baking pans. Let pralines cool until set, about 30 minutes. Serve immediately or store in an airtight container for up to 1 week.

BRIGHT IDEA! When choosing chocolate for baking, select bars teeming with cocoa butter and no added fats, such as Ghirardelli's 60 percent bittersweet and milk chocolate baking bars.

A cinch to prepare, these bite-size truffles up the ante on plain peanut butter cups.

Vanilla bean makes these caramels extra special.

CHOCOLATE–PEANUT BUTTER TRUFFLES

Makes 48 truffles ***Working time*** 45 min.
Total time 5 hr.

8   ounces bittersweet chocolate, chopped
1   cup heavy cream
½   cup smooth peanut butter
½   teaspoon vanilla extract
¼   teaspoon salt
⅓   cups cocoa
½   cup finely chopped peanuts

1. Place bittersweet chocolate, chopped, in a medium heat-safe bowl. Set aside.
2. In a medium saucepan over low heat, cook heavy cream until it just begins to boil, then immediately pour over chocolate. Let sit for 1 minute. Stir until chocolate is melted and mixture is thick and smooth. Stir in smooth peanut butter, vanilla extract, and salt. Pour into a shallow baking pan and refrigerate until set, 4 to 6 hours.
3. Spoon chocolate–peanut butter mixture, by the tablespoon, into your hand and roll into balls. Place on a parchment-lined baking pan and return to refrigerator for 20 to 30 minutes.
4. Place cocoa and finely chopped peanuts in separate shallow dishes. Roll ½ of the truffles in cocoa and the other ½ in peanuts, constantly shaping each ball as you work. Keep refrigerated until serving.

CHOCOLATE-DIPPED VANILLA CARAMELS

Makes 3 dozen candies ***Working time*** 45 min.
Total time 1 hr. 30 min., plus cooling

1   cup sugar
1   cup heavy cream
½   cup unsalted butter
1   cup light corn syrup
1   vanilla bean, split lengthwise, seeds scraped
1   teaspoon vanilla extract
9   ounces semisweet chocolate, chopped
1½ teaspoons vegetable shortening
1   tablespoon Maldon salt

1. Make the caramels: Line 3 baking pans with parchment. Lightly coat both the lined pans and a 2-cup heat-resistant glass liquid measuring cup with vegetable oil. Set aside. Place the sugar in a medium nonstick saucepan over high heat, and cook, without stirring, until ½ the sugar has melted and the edges are bubbling. Stir until liquefied and light caramel in color—about 1 minute. Remove from the heat and add the cream. The mixture will foam up and harden. Add the butter, corn syrup, and vanilla bean seeds. Return to the stovetop and cook over low heat until caramel dissolves—about 45 minutes. Increase heat to medium-high and cook until the syrup reaches firm ball stage (243°F on a candy thermometer). Add the vanilla extract. Very carefully transfer the hot caramel to the prepared measuring cup, allowing the foam to subside as you pour. Pour about a teaspoon of caramel onto the prepared pan, forming a 2-inch-diameter circle. Repeat with remaining caramel, spreading lightly with the back of an oiled spoon to form circles as the caramel hardens. Let cool completely.
2. Dip the caramels: Melt the chocolate and shortening in a double boiler over barely simmering water, until melted. Dip ½ of each caramel into the chocolate and return to the prepared pan. Sprinkle with the salt and freeze for a minute to set. Store at room temperature in an airtight container layered with parchment for up to 1 week.

SPRINGERLE COOKIES

Makes 3 dozen 2½-inch round cookies
Working time 1 hr. *Total time* 2 hr., *plus sitting time*

3¾	cups all-purpose flour
¼	teaspoon salt
¼	teaspoon baking powder
4	large eggs, at room temperature
1¾	cups sugar
1	teaspoon lemon extract
1	teaspoon anise seed, optional Luster dust, in assorted colors

1. Line 2 baking sheets with parchment paper. Combine 3¼ cups flour, salt, and baking powder in a medium bowl, and set aside. Beat the eggs and sugar in a large bowl with an electric mixer set on high speed until pale and doubled in volume—about 3 minutes. Add extract and beat to combine. Stir in the flour mixture, and anise seeds, if desired.

2. Sprinkle up to ½ cup flour on a clean work surface. Transfer the dough to the surface and knead in the flour until dough is soft and smooth. Form a rough ball, divide the dough in half, and wrap in plastic to prevent drying. Roll out the remaining dough to ¼-inch thickness. Lightly dust your choice of rubber stamps or springerle pin with flour to prevent sticking. Press the stamps or roll the pin to imprint the dough and use a cutter to cut out pieces.

3. Using a spatula, transfer the pieces to the prepared baking sheets and let sit uncovered 10 to 12 hours. Heat oven to 300° F. Bake the cookies, 1 sheet at a time, on the center rack of the oven until almost firm and not colored—25 to 30 minutes.

4. Transfer cookies to a wire rack to cool. Lightly dampen luster dust with lemon extract in a small dish, until a thick paste forms. Paint the cooled cookies with a light dabbing motion, using a small paintbrush. Allow the "paint" about 5 to 10 minutes to dry completely. Store Springerle in an airtight container.

FOR MORE COOKIES, SEE THESE RECIPES IN CHAPTER 5, HOMEMADE GIFTS FROM THE KITCHEN

p. 130

Cranberry, Pistachio, and Chocolate-Chunk Cookies

Linzer Tart Christmas Trees

Red-and-White Marbled Cookies

Pressed Flower Cookies

Chocolate-Filled Stars

p. 133

Sugar-Cookie Buttons

p. 135

Cinnamon-Sugar Lattice Cookies

p. 139

Roly Polys

Jam Thumbprints

Red-and-Whites

Raspberry Bars

◇◇◇◇◇

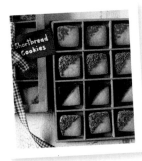

p. 136

Shortbread Cookies

p. 140

Gingerbread Animals

Photo Credits

Index